GLOBAL FOREST RESOURCES ASSESSMENT 2015

How are the world's forests changing?

FOOD AND AGRICULTURE ORGANIZATION OF THE UNITED NATIONS

Rome, 2015

The Global Forest Resources Assessment

Sustainably managed forests provide essential goods and services and thus play a vital part in sustainable development. Reliable and up-to-date information on the state of forest resources is crucial to support decision-making for investment and policymaking in forestry and sustainable development.

FAO, at the request of its member countries, regularly monitors the world´s forests and their management and uses through the Global Forest Resources Assessment (FRA). More information on the FRA 2015 process, other publications and online database is available on the FRA web site (www.fao.org/forestry/fra).

The FRA process is coordinated by the Forestry Department at FAO headquarters in Rome in coordination with partners in the Collaborative Forest Resources Questionnaire (CFRQ). These six partners are: the Central African Forest Commission (COMIFAC/ OFAC), FAO, FOREST EUROPE, the International Tropical Timber Organization (ITTO), the Montréal Process, and the United Nations Economic Commission for Europe (UNECE).

ISBN 978-92-5-108821-0

Contents

Acknowledgements

The *Global Forest Resources Assessment 2015: How are the world's forests changing?* is the product of many contributors and supporters. FAO acknowledges with gratitude the contributions of the governments of Canada, Finland, Japan, the United States of America and the European Union for financial support during the process of preparing FRA 2015. The financial support of Canada, FOREST EUROPE and the International Tropical Timber Organization (ITTO) in producing this report are also much appreciated. Remote sensing support was provided by the European Commission Joint Research Centre (JRC).

Global forest resource reporting is not possible without contributions from the nearly 300 FRA national correspondents and alternates who are appointed by their governments to prepare responses to the FRA/CFRQ questionnaire. National investments in data collection, workshops and report writing were substantial and were the foundation of the 155 country reports in FRA 2015. Regional or global workshops were co-sponsored by FAO/UNECE, Canada, Finland, India, Japan, Mexico, Thailand and the United States of America and were an important part of the FRA 2015 process.

This report was written by K. MacDicken, Ö. Jonsson, L.Piña, S. Maulo, Y. Adikari, M. Garzuglia, E. Lindquist, G. Reams and R. D'Annunzio. Technical support was provided by P. Mundhenk and C. Boitani. Publications support services were provided by M. Palermo and L. Marinaro. D. Taylor edited the report and S. Lapstun provided editorial services and production coordination. Design and layout was done by F. Dicarlo. The quality of data and of the report were improved with reviews by CFRQ partners, FAO Forestry Department staff and peer reviewers to whom we are grateful.

Foreword

The contributions of forests to the well-being of humankind are extraordinarily vast and far-reaching. Forests play a fundamental role in combating rural poverty, ensuring food security and providing decent livelihoods; they offer promising mid-term green growth opportunities; and they deliver vital long-term environmental services, such as clean air and water, conservation of biodiversity and mitigation of climate change.

Forestry has an important place in FAO's Strategic Framework, which strongly promotes an integrated approach to addressing the major problems that concern food production, rural development, land use and sustainable management of natural resources.

However, in order to manage our forests wisely for the benefit of current and future generations, it is vital to have a clear understanding of the situation of the world's forests and ongoing trends.

The *Global Forest Resources Assessment* (FRA) allows us to do exactly that. Since the first FRA was published in 1948, FAO has reported periodically on the situation of the world's forests, serving the international community with the best information and techniques available.

FRA 2015 arrives in a decisive year for forests and sustainable development. This year the development agenda towards 2030 is being defined, including the adoption of new Sustainable Development Goals (SDGs). Forests and their role in protecting and restoring terrestrial ecosystems and their services are essential for the post-2015 development agenda.

A global and inclusive climate change agreement – in which forests are a key part – is also expected to be reached at the Conference of the Parties of the United Nations Framework Convention on Climate Change to be held in Paris in December 2015. The year 2015 also features the XIV World Forestry Congress in Durban, the biggest international forest event of this decade – to be held in Africa for the first time – where we are honoured to launch FRA 2015.

FRA 2015 shows a very encouraging tendency towards a reduction in the rates of deforestation and carbon emissions from forests and increases in capacity for sustainable forest management. The reliability of the information collected has also improved enormously – presently national forest inventories apply to some 81 percent of global forest area, a substantial increase over the past 10 years.

Two broad conclusions can be drawn: 1) we have a wealth of reliable information today on the situation of the world's forests; and 2) the direction of change is positive, with many impressive examples of progress in all regions of the world. However this positive trend needs to be strengthened, especially in the countries that are lagging behind.

FRA 2015 is the result of countries' collective efforts, including some 300 national correspondents, partners and FAO. The Collaborative Forest Resources Questionnaire, implemented by 6 partners and processes, covers 88 percent of the world's forests. This ongoing collaborative effort is improving data consistency while reducing countries' reporting burdens. In addition, FRA 2015 has incorporated data quality indicators for the first time.

The Assessment is available in a range of formats, including the present synthesis document, a desk reference containing summary tables, a special issue of the journal *Forest Ecology and Management*, and the Forest Land Use Data Explorer – an online database that integrates FRA data with other FAO data sources.

FRA 2015 is a major step forward. I encourage you to take full advantage of the information included in this report.

José Graziano da Silva
FAO Director-General

Acronyms

C&I	Criteria and Indicators
CFRQ	Collaborative Forest Resources Questionnaire
COMIFAC/OFAC	Central African Forest Commission/Observatoire des Forêts d'Afrique Centrale
FAO	Food and Agriculture Organization of the United Nations
FMP	forest management plan
FRA	Global Forest Resources Assessment (FAO)
FRIMS	Forest Resources Information Management System
FSC	Forest Stewardship Council
GDP	gross domestic product
GFRM	Global Forest Resources Model
GHG	greenhouse gas
HCVF	high conservation value forests
ISIC	International Standard Industrial Classification of all Economic Activities
ITTO	International Tropical Timber Organization
JRC	European Commission Joint Research Centre
MODIS	Moderate Resolution Imaging Spectroradiometer satellite
NACE	Statistical classification of economic activities in the European Community
NFI	national forest inventory
NGO	non-governmental organization
NWFP	non-wood forest product
PCCL	partial canopy cover loss
PEFC	Programme for Endorsement of Forest Certification
PFE	permanent forest estate
REDD	Reducing Emissions from Deforestation and Forest Degradation
SFM	sustainable forest management
SIDS	Small Island Developing States
UNECE	United Nations Economic Commission for Europe
UNFCCC	United Nations Framework Convention on Climate Change
VCF	Vegetation Continuous Fields

1990-2015:
Twenty-five years
in review

Forests and forest management have changed substantially over the past 25 years. Overall, this period has seen a series of positive results. Even though, globally, the extent of the world's forest continues to decline as human populations continue to grow and demand for food and land increases, the rate of net forest loss has been cut by over 50 percent. At the same time, the attention paid to sustainable forest management has never been higher: more land is designated as permanent forest, more measurement, monitoring, reporting, planning and stakeholder involvement is taking place, and the legal framework for sustaining forest management is nearly universal. Larger areas are being designated for conservation of biodiversity at the same time as forests are meeting increasing demand for forest products and services.

In 1990 the world had 4 128 million ha of forest; by 2015 this area has decreased to 3 999 million ha. This is a change from 31.6 percent of global land area in 1990 to 30.6 percent[1] in 2015. Yet deforestation, or forest conversion, is more complicated than that. Globally, forest gains and losses occur continuously, and are very difficult to monitor even with high resolution satellite imagery. Natural forest and planted forest area change dynamics differ – and vary dramatically across national circumstances and forest types.

We can describe forest area change as a process of gain (forest expansion) and loss (deforestation). Change in total forest area provides a picture of how all forest resources combined are changing. Natural forest change is perhaps a better indicator of natural habitat and biodiversity dynamics. Change in planted forest helps us to understand shifts in the forest product mix from natural and planted forests.

There was a net loss of some 129 million ha of forest (natural and planted) from 1990 to 2015, representing an annual rate of –0.13 percent and a total area about the size of South Africa. Still, this should be understood in context: the net annual rate of loss has slowed from –0.18 percent in the 1990s to –0.08 over the last five-year period. Between 2010 and 2015 there was an annual loss of 7.6 million ha and an annual gain of 4.3 million ha per year, resulting in a net annual decrease in forest area of 3.3 million ha per year.

The biggest forest area loss occurred in the tropics, particularly in South America and Africa, although the rate of loss in those areas has decreased substantially in the past five years. Average per capita forest area declined from 0.8 ha to 0.6 ha per person from 1990 to 2015. While per capita forest area decline is greatest in the tropics and subtropics, it is occurring in every climatic domain (except in the temperate domain) as populations increase and forest land is converted to agriculture and other land uses.

The bulk of the world's forest is natural forest,[2] amounting to 93 percent of global forest area or 3.7 billion ha in 2015. From 2010 to 2015, natural forest decreased by a net 6.6 million ha per year (8.8 million ha of loss and 2.2 million ha of natural forest gain). This is a reduction in net annual natural forest loss from 8.5 million ha per year (1990 to 2000) to 6.6 million ha per year (2010 to 2015). While the Global Forest Resources Assessment (FRA) does not report deforestation directly due to the complexity of collecting deforestation statistics, the area of natural forest loss is a very good proxy.

Most natural forest falls into the category of "other naturally regenerated forest" (65 percent); the remaining 35 percent is reported as primary forest. Since 1990, 38 million ha of primary forest have been reported as modified or cleared by countries reporting in all years (although not all countries report in all years). This does not necessarily mean that this forest is converted to other land uses. Primary forest, when modified but not cleared, changes into other naturally regenerated (secondary) forest and in some cases planted forest. The total reported primary forest area has increased from 1990 to 2015, largely because more countries now report on this forest characteristic. Some countries have reported increases in primary forest because national old-growth forest categories have been reclassified (e.g. Costa Rica, Japan, Malaysia, Russian Federation and the United States of America).

Planted forest area has increased by over 110 million ha since 1990 and accounts for 7 percent of the world's forest area. The average annual rate of increase between 1990 and 2000 was 3.6 million ha. The rate peaked at 5.2 million ha per year for the period 2000 to 2010 and slowed to 3.1 million ha (2010–2015) per year, as planting decreased in East Asia, Europe, North America, South and Southeast Asia. During this period planted forests increased by a net 3.1 million ha per year (3.5 million ha of planted forest gain and 0.4 million ha of planted forest loss).

The production/consumption of wood in general has increased throughout the period while reliance on woodfuel has remained large. In 1990 annual wood removals amounted to 2.8 billion m³, of which 41 percent was for woodfuel; in 2011 annual wood removals amounted to 3.0 billion m³, of which 49 percent was for woodfuel. Both the proportion of wood removals used for fuel and the total amount of wood used for fuel have increased.

---

[1] Calculated on the basis of 2015 land area.

[2] The sum of primary forest and other naturally regenerated forest.

©FAO/Jim Ball

In 2015 about 30 percent of the world's forest was designated as production forest, a slight increase from 1990 (28 percent). Forest designated as multiple use increased from 23 percent of total forest area to 26 percent between 1990–2015. Multiple-use forest provides timber, range, non-wood forest products, water, recreation and wildlife management values. These increases in proportion come in part from stable designations and decreasing total forest areas.

The conservation of biodiversity represents the primary management objective for 13 percent of the world's forests and, since 1990, 150 million ha of forest have been added to the conservation category. Forests designated for the protection of soil and water represent 25 percent of the total forest area.

Reduced forest stocking is less visible but it is an important reality in many parts of the world. Over the past 25 years global carbon stocks in forest biomass decreased by almost 17.4 gigatonnes (Gt). This reduction was mainly driven by conversion to other land uses and forest degradation.

Progress towards sustainable forest management (SFM) has been substantial over the last 25 years. Ninety-nine percent of the world's forests are covered by both policies and legislation supporting SFM at national and subnational level. Most countries offer opportunities for stakeholders to provide input to national policy processes – although with varying degrees of efficacy. Progress has been higher in the temperate areas and highly variable in the tropics where the capacity to utilize or enforce SFM policies, laws and regulations remains uneven.

Forest resource data are being generated now at a greater frequency than any other time in history. As of 2014, 112 countries had national forest inventories, including some 77 percent of the world's forest area covered by national forest inventories that were either completed or initiated since 2010. The area covered by national forest inventory (NFI) between 1970 and 2014 is 3.3 billion ha or 82 percent of total forest area. This represents a very large investment by governments in recent years to better understand their forest resources. A high proportion of forest area (92 percent) is also reported through national reporting systems – although forest reporting is lagging behind in the tropics and in low-income countries.

The area of forest under management plans has also increased. In 1953, forest management plans covered around 27 percent of production forest area, in 2010 it was 70 percent of production forest area. By 2010 the area under management plan was 52 percent of the total forest area, equally split between production and conservation purposes. The majority of these plans require social and community involvement specifications and the delineation of high conservation value forests (HCVF). More than half of all areas covered by forest management plans have requirements for soil and water protection.

The area under forest management certification has continued to increase, from 18 million ha under internationally verified certification in 2000 to some 438 million ha in 2014. About 90 percent of the total area certified in 2014 is in the temperate and boreal climatic domains although there has also been growth, albeit at a slower pace, in the tropics and subtropics.

The forest sector currently employs about 1.7 percent of the global workforce (see *State of the World's Forests (SOFO)* report, FAO, 2014), of which 0.4 percent work in the forest. The rest are in transport, processing and manufacturing activities outside the forest.

Most forests remain publicly owned, but forest ownership by communities and individuals has increased. The proportion of privately-owned forests has increased from 13 percent in 1990 to 19 percent of the total forest area in 2010. Most of this increase in private ownership has been in upper middle-income countries. However, for countries that have private forest it is a much larger proportion - in 1990 nearly 26 percent of forest in these countries was owned privately, a number that increased to 30 percent in 2010. Public forest management rights held by private companies have increased substantially (from 3 percent to 15 percent of public forest area) from 1990 to 2010.

Over the past 25 years the world's forests have changed in dynamic and diverse ways. Countries have more knowledge of their forest resources than ever before and as a result we have a better picture of global forest change. The rate of forest area loss is declining and the indicators for sustainable forest management reveal positive progress in forest management. At the same time, important challenges remain. The existence of sound policies, legislation and regulation is not always coupled with effective incentives or enforcement. Unsustainable forest practices and forest conversion clearly persist – despite increased efforts – and the benefits from forest utilization in some countries do not effectively reach local communities. FAO's *Global Forest Resources Assessment 2015* (FRA 2015) documents both substantial progress in forest management and a need for continued efforts to sustain forest management for the benefit of current and future generations.

Introducing
FRA 2015

Working together

The first FAO *Global Forest Resources Assessment* was published in 1948. It comprised five indicators and its main focus was to assess the availability of timber. Since then, global assessments have evolved to respond to increasing information needs, including many descriptors of the forest resource and sustainable forest management. FRA 2015 is the result of contributions from 155 countries and the hard work of national correspondents who prepared country reports that present government forest statistics in a common format.

When FRA began in 1948, FAO was the only organization collecting and reporting global forest resource information. Today there are many international and regional organizations involved in measuring, monitoring and reporting forest resource data, mostly using remote sensing with little or no information other than tree cover area estimates. In 2011, six international organizations and processes[3] came together to create the Collaborative Forest Resources Questionnaire (CFRQ), representing some 100 countries and 88 percent of the world's forest area. These organizations now jointly collect data on over 60 percent of the total number of variables collected through the FRA process. These data are then shared among the CFRQ partners so that countries are asked only once for this information. In other words, the data are collected once and used many times. This both reduces the reporting burden and increases data consistency across organizations. The CFRQ partnership has in the process also helped to standardize definitions and timing of data collection.

Beyond the CFRQ, partnership has also been crucial in the area of remote sensing. The global remote sensing survey was conducted with over 200 specialists from about 100 countries. In addition, a close working relationship with the European Commission Joint Research Centre (JRC) has resulted in the sharing of both technical advances and the workload of global forest change analysis of Landsat data.

A quick guide to the data

The FRA/CFRQ 2015 dataset and the analyses have some unique attributes that should be considered when using this document. For more information on where the data have come from please see the data sources section at the end of this document.

A few points to keep in mind:

1. Summary tables for all variables collected in FRA 2015 are presented in the FRA 2015 Desk Reference which can be found at http://www.fao.org/forestry/fra/fra2015/en/.

2. A more detailed set of analyses are presented in independently peer-reviewed papers in the journal *Forest Ecology and Management* at http://www.sciencedirect.com/science/journal/03781127/352.

3. Data can also be accessed through the Forest Land Use Data Explorer (FLUDE) website, which provides integrated access to FRA 2015 and other land use related data. It can be accessed from the FRA 2015 link above.

4. Specific analytical methods may vary by variable or category and are summarized at http://www.fao.org/forestry/fra/76872/en/.

5. The main categories used for the analyses are:
   5.1. *Region and subregion.* These are the same geographic region and subregion groupings used in FRA 2010.
   5.2. *Climatic domain.* FRA country data are classified by dominant climatic domains (Tropical, Subtropical, Temperate and Boreal) for each country (http://www.fao.org/forestry/fra/76872/en/). In some cases, particularly in northern latitudes, this means that not all climatic domains are represented. For example, the United States of America has boreal, temperate and subtropical forest, but because the largest forest category is temperate it is reported as the temperate climatic domain. There are fewer examples of this occurring for countries with tropical and subtropical domains.
   5.3. *Income categories.* These analyses use World Bank income categories that are updated every July. The analyses used for FRA 2015 use the 2013 classifications at http://data.worldbank.org/news/new-country-classifications. These categories cover most countries and territories, but not all. This means that total area values summed across income categories will not be the same as the totals for all countries and territories - but the differences are small. Certainly there are also some countries that have moved from one income category to another between 1990 and 2013; these changes are difficult to track and are not addressed in these analyses.

6. FRA 2015 provides indicators of data quality, introducing a Tier system in which most variables are labelled by countries according to a pre-established set of definitions. The main purpose of the Tiers is to identify indicator data quality, primarily age of the data and nature of the original data source. Tier 3 is the most recent and most robust data source, Tier 2 older and less complete, and Tier 1 an expert estimate (see data sources section).

---

[3] Central African Forest Commission/Observatoire des Forêts d'Afrique Centrale (COMIFAC/OFAC), FAO, FOREST EUROPE, International Tropical Timber Organization (ITTO), Montréal Process, United Nations Economic Commission for Europe (UNECE).

Statistical profiles

Global profiles (234 countries and territories)

Variable/unit/year	Total	Direction of change[a]
FOREST AREA AND CHARACTERISTICS		
Forest area (million ha, 2015)	3 999	↓
Area of other wooded land (million ha, 2015)	1 204	↓
Area of other land with tree cover (million ha, 2015)	284	↑
Average annual reforestation (million ha, 2010)	27	↑
Natural forest (million ha, 2015)[b]	3 713	↓
Primary forest (million ha, 2015)	1 277	↓
Other naturally regenerated forest (million ha, 2015)	2 337	↓
Planted forest (million ha, 2015)	290	↑
Net forest change (million ha, 2010-2015)	-17	NA
Net annual forest change (million ha, 2010-2015)	-3	NA
Net natural forest change (million ha, 2010-2015)[b]	-33	NA
Net annual natural forest change (million ha, 2010-2015)[b]	-7	NA
Net planted forest change (million ha, 2010-2015)	15	NA
Net annual planted forest change (million ha, 2010-2015)	3	NA
PRODUCTION		
Forest growing stock (billion m³, 2015)	431	↑
Carbon in above- and below-ground biomass (Gt, 2015)	250	↓
Production forest (million ha, 2015)[c]	1 187	↑
Multiple use forest (million ha, 2015)[c]	1 049	↑
Total wood removals (million m³, 2011)	2 997	↑
PROTECTIVE FUNCTIONS AND SELECTIVE ECOSYSTEM SERVICES		
Protection of soil and water (million ha, 2015)[c]	1 015	↑
Environmental services, cultural or spiritual values (million ha, 2015)[c]	1 163	↑
BIODIVERSITY AND CONSERVATION		
Conservation of biodiversity (million ha, 2015)[c]	524	↑
Forest area within protected areas (million ha, 2015)[c]	651	↑

Variable/unit/year	Total	Direction of change[a]
DISTURBANCES		
Area with invasive woody species (million ha, 2010)	79	↑
Average annual forest area burned (million ha, 2003-2012)	50	NA
Forest area with reduction in canopy cover (million ha, 2000-2010)	185	NA
MEASURING PROGRESS TOWARD SUSTAINABLE FOREST MANAGEMENT (SFM)		
Countries with policies supporting sustainable forest management (latest available year)	148	NA
Countries with legislation and regulation supporting SFM (latest available year)	145	NA
Forest area in permanent forest land use (million ha, 2010)	2 166	NA
Forest area with management plan (million ha, 2010)	2 100	NA
Percent forest area with management plans monitored annually (2015)	39%	NA
Forest area certified under an international scheme (million ha, 2014)[c]	438	↑
Forest area certified under a domestic scheme (million ha, 2012)[c]	59	↑
Countries with national stakeholder Platform (latest available year)	126	NA
Forest area monitored using remote sensing or aerial imagery (million ha, 2010)	2 277	NA
Forest area covered by Criteria and Indicator reporting (million ha, latest available year)	3 078	NA
Forest area reported through periodic national state of forest reports (million ha, latest available year)	3 530	NA
OWNERSHIP		
Public (million ha, 2010)	2 969	↓
Private (million ha, 2010)	774	↑
Unknown (million ha, 2010)	141	↓
ECONOMICS / LIVELIHOOD		
In-forest employment (million persons, 2010)	12.7	↓
Gross value added from in-forest activities (billion USD, latest year)	150	NA
Gross value added from the forest sector (*SOFO 2014*, billion USD, 2011)	606	NA

[a] Calculated as: sum of 1990 or earliest year values – sum of latest year values.

[b] Natural forest is calculated as the sum of other naturally regenerated and primary forest areas reported by countries or when these data were missing natural forest was calculated as total forest area – planted forest area.

[c] Not mutually exclusive variable that may overlap with other reported area values.

Regional profiles

Africa (58 countries and territories)		
Variable/unit/year	**Total**	**Direction of change[a]**
Forest area (million ha, 2015)	624	↓
Primary forest (million ha, 2015)	135	↓
Planted forest (million ha, 2015)	16	↑
Net forest change (million ha, 2010-2015)	-14.2	NA
Net annual forest change (million ha, 2010-2015)	-2.8	NA
Net natural forest change (million ha, 2010-2015)[b]	-15.6	NA
Net annual natural forest change (million ha, 2010-2015)[b]	-3.1	NA
Net planted forest change (million ha, 2010-2015)	1	NA
Net annual planted forest change (million ha, 2010-2015)	0.2	NA
Forest growing stock (billion m³ over bark, 2015)	78	↓
Carbon in above- and below-ground biomass (Gt, 2015)	59	↓
Production forest (million ha, 2015)[c]	165	↓
Multiple-use forest (million ha, 2015)[c]	133	↑
Total wood removals (million m³, 2011)	614	↑
Protection of soil and water (million ha, 2015)[c]	50	↑
Environmental services, cultural or spiritual values (million ha, 2015)[c]	67	↓
Conservation of biodiversity (million ha, 2015)[c]	92	↑
Forest area within protected areas (million ha, 2015)[c]	101	↑
Average annual forest area burned (million ha, 2003-2012)	17	NA
Forest area with reduction in canopy cover (million ha, 2000-2010)	50	NA
Forest area with management plan (million ha, 2010)	140	NA
Forest area certified under an international scheme (million ha, 2014)	6	↑
Public ownership (million ha, 2010)	535	↓
Private ownership (million ha, 2010)	71	↑
Unknown ownership (million ha, 2010)	2	↓
In-forest employment (thousand persons, 2010)	1 109	↑

Asia (48 countries and territories)		
Variable/unit/year	**Total**	**Direction of change[a]**
Forest area (million ha, 2015)	593	↑
Primary forest (million ha, 2015)	117	↑
Planted forest (million ha, 2015)	129	↑
Net forest change (million ha, 2010-2015)	4	NA
Net annual forest change (million ha, 2010-2015)	0.8	NA
Net natural forest change (million ha, 2010-2015)[b]	-5.1	NA
Net annual natural forest change (million ha, 2010-2015)[b]	-1	NA
Net planted forest change (million ha, 2010-2015)	9.1	NA
Net annual planted forest change (million ha, 2010-2015)	1.8	NA
Forest growing stock (billion m³ over bark, 2015)	51	↓
Carbon in above- and below-ground biomass (Gt, 2015)	34	↓
Production forest (million ha, 2015)[c]	247	↑
Multiple-use forest (million ha, 2015)[c]	129	↓
Total wood removals (million m³, 2011)	780	↑
Protection of soil and water (million ha, 2015)[c]	195	↑
Environmental services, cultural or spiritual values (million ha, 2015)[c]	43	↑
Conservation of biodiversity (million ha, 2015)[c]	86	↑
Forest area within protected areas (million ha, 2015)[c]	115	↑
Average annual forest area burned (million ha, 2003-2012)	1	NA
Forest area with reduction in canopy cover (million ha, 2000-2010)	54	NA
Forest area with management plan (million ha, 2010)	410	NA
Forest area certified under an international scheme (million ha, 2014)	14	↑
Public ownership (million ha, 2010)	453	↓
Private ownership (million ha, 2010)	134	↑
Unknown ownership (million ha, 2010)	1	↓
In-forest employment (thousand persons, 2010)	9 939	↓

Europe (50 countries and territories)		
Variable/unit/year	**Total**	**Direction of change[a]**
Forest area (million ha, 2015)	1015	↑
Primary forest (million ha, 2015)	277	↑
Planted forest (million ha, 2015)	82	↑
Net forest change (million ha, 2010-2015)	1.9	NA
Net annual forest change (million ha, 2010-2015)	0.4	NA
Net natural forest change (million ha, 2010-2015)[b]	0.2	NA
Net annual natural forest change (million ha, 2010-2015)[b]	0	NA
Net planted forest change (million ha, 2010-2015)	0.9	NA
Net annual planted forest change (million ha, 2010-2015)	0.2	NA
Forest growing stock (billion m³ over bark, 2015)	114	↑
Carbon in above- and below-ground biomass (Gt, 2015)	45	↑
Production forest (million ha, 2015)[c]	511	↓
Multiple-use forest (million ha, 2015)[c]	238	↓
Total wood removals (million m³, 2011)	681	↓
Protection of soil and water (million ha, 2015)[c]	123	↑
Environmental services, cultural or spiritual values (million ha, 2015)[c]	122	↑
Conservation of biodiversity (million ha, 2015)[c]	53	↑
Forest area within protected areas (million ha, 2015)[c]	46	↑
Average annual forest area burned (million ha, 2003-2012)	2	NA
Forest area with reduction in canopy cover (million ha, 2000-2010)	18	NA
Forest area with management plan (million ha, 2010)	949	NA
Forest area certified under an international scheme (million ha, 2014)	167	↑
Public ownership (million ha, 2010)	897	=
Private ownership (million ha, 2010)	108	↑
Unknown ownership (million ha, 2010)	8	↑
In-forest employment (thousand persons, 2010)	671	↓

[a] Calculated as: sum of 1990 or earliest year values - sum of latest year values.

[b] Natural forest is calculated as the sum of other naturally regenerated and primary forest areas reported by countries or when these data were missing natural forest was calculated as total forest area - planted forest area.

[c] Not mutually exclusive variable that may overlap with other reported area values.

North and Central America (39 countries and territories)			Oceania (25 countries and territories)			South America (14 countries and territories)		
Variable/unit/year	Total	Direction of change[a]	Variable/unit/year	Total	Direction of change[a]	Variable/unit/year	Total	Direction of change[a]
Forest area (million ha, 2015)	751	↓	Forest area (million ha, 2015)	174	↓	Forest area (million ha, 2015)	842	↓
Primary forest (million ha, 2015)	320	↓	Primary forest (million ha, 2015)	27	↓	Primary forest (million ha, 2015)	400	↓
Planted forest (million ha, 2015)	43	↑	Planted forest (million ha, 2015)	4	↑	Planted forest (million ha, 2015)	15	↑
Net forest change (million ha, 2010-2015)	0.4	NA	Net forest change (million ha, 2010-2015)	1.5	NA	Net forest change (million ha, 2010-2015)	-10.1	NA
Net annual forest change (million ha, 2010-2015)	0.1	NA	Net annual forest change (million ha, 2010-2015)	0.3	NA	Net annual forest change (million ha, 2010-2015)	-2	NA
Net natural forest change (million ha, 2010-2015)[b]	-2.2	NA	Net natural forest change (million ha, 2010-2015)[b]	1.4	NA	Net natural forest change (million ha, 2010-2015)[b]	-11.9	NA
Net annual natural forest change (million ha, 2010-2015)[b]	0.4	NA	Net annual natural forest change (million ha, 2010-2015)[b]	0.3	NA	Net annual natural forest change (million ha, 2010-2015)[b]	-2.4	NA
Net planted forest change (million ha, 2010-2015)	2.5	NA	Net planted forest change (million ha, 2010-2015)	0.1	NA	Net planted forest change (million ha, 2010-2015)	1.8	NA
Net annual planted forest change (million ha, 2010-2015)	0.5	NA	Net annual planted forest change (million ha, 2010-2015)	0	NA	Net annual planted forest change (million ha, 2010-2015)	0.4	NA
Forest growing stock (billion m³ over bark, 2015)	49	↑	Forest growing stock (billion m³ over bark, 2015)	10	↑	Forest growing stock (billion m³ over bark, 2015)	129	↓
Carbon in above- and below-ground biomass (Gt, 2015)	22	↓	Carbon in above- and below-ground biomass (Gt, 2015)	8	↑	Carbon in above- and below-ground biomass (Gt, 2015)	82	↓
Production forest (million ha, 2015)[c]	124	↑	Production forest (million ha, 2015)[c]	13	↑	Production forest (million ha, 2015)[c]	127	↑
Multiple-use forest (million ha, 2015)[c]	391	↓	Multiple-use forest (million ha, 2015)[c]	54	↑	Multiple-use forest (million ha, 2015)[c]	104	↑
Total wood removals (million m³, 2011)	513	↓	Total wood removals (million m³, 2011)	63	↑	Total wood removals (million m³, 2011)	346	=
Protection of soil and water (million ha, 2015)[c]	534	↑	Protection of soil and water (million ha, 2015)[c]	37	↑	Protection of soil and water (million ha, 2015)[c]	76	↑
Environmental services, cultural or spiritual values (million ha, 2015)[c]	642	↑	Environmental services, cultural or spiritual values (million ha, 2015)[c]	123	↓	Environmental services, cultural or spiritual values (million ha, 2015)[c]	166	↑
Conservation of biodiversity (million ha, 2015)[c]	127	↑	Conservation of biodiversity (million ha, 2015)[c]	36	↑	Conservation of biodiversity (million ha, 2015)[c]	130	↑
Forest area within protected areas (million ha, 2015)[c]	75	↑	Forest area within protected areas (million ha, 2015)[c]	27	↑	Forest area within protected areas (million ha, 2015)[c]	287	↑
Average annual forest area burned (million ha, 2003-2012)	4	NA	Average annual forest area burned (million ha, 2003-2012)	4	NA	Average annual forest area burned (million ha, 2003-2012)	21	NA
Forest area with reduction in canopy cover (million ha, 2000-2010)	10	NA	Forest area with reduction in canopy cover (million ha, 2000-2010)	5	NA	Forest area with reduction in canopy cover (million ha, 2000-2010)	47	NA
Forest area with management plan (million ha, 2010)	430	NA	Forest area with management plan (million ha, 2010)	46	NA	Forest area with management plan (million ha, 2010)	125	NA
Forest area certified under an international scheme (million ha, 2014)	222	↑	Forest area certified under an international scheme (million ha, 2014)	13	↑	Forest area certified under an international scheme (million ha, 2014)	15	↑
Public ownership (million ha, 2010)	458	↑	Public ownership (million ha, 2010)	97	↓	Public ownership (million ha, 2010)	528	↓
Private ownership (million ha, 2010)	244	↑	Private ownership (million ha, 2010)	72	↓	Private ownership (million ha, 2010)	145	↑
Unknown ownership (million ha, 2010)	34	↑	Unknown ownership (million ha, 2010)	1	↑	Unknown ownership (million ha, 2010)	95	↑
In-forest employment (thousand persons, 2010)	186	↓	In-forest employment (thousand persons, 2010)	16	=	In-forest employment (thousand persons, 2010)	734	↑

[a] Calculated as: sum of 1990 or earliest year values – sum of latest year values.

[b] Natural forest is calculated as the sum of other naturally regenerated and primary forest areas reported by countries or when these data were missing natural forest was calculated as total forest area – planted forest area.

[c] Not mutually exclusive variable that may overlap with other reported area values.

Sustainability indicators

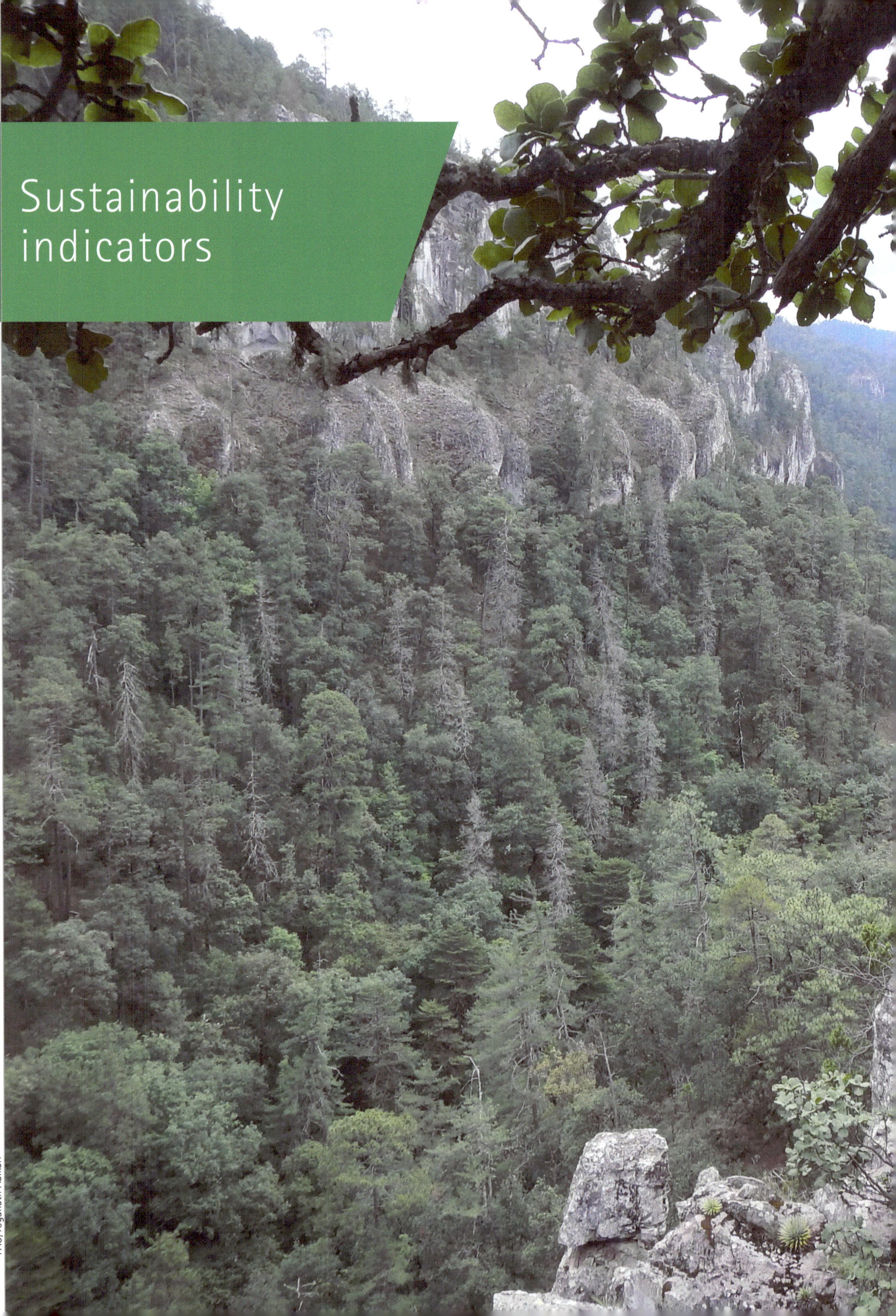

©FAO/Yoganath Adikari

Managing forests responsibly and sustainably requires a balanced approach encompassing the three pillars of sustainability – economic, social and environmental. Measuring progress in each of these broad areas in a meaningful way is complex and in many cases not fully achievable, even in countries that have the resources to collect relevant data. However, indicators that measure progress provide a guide to how management and investment decisions can be adapted to meet the needs and expectations of current and future generations.

What are they?

Sustainability indicators are science-based measures that provide a consistent approach to define, assess, monitor and report progress on sustainable forest management to a wide range of stakeholders and institutions, including governments, the private sector, NGOs, donor organizations, researchers and the public. Sustainability indicators can be useful to identify the changes in forest management practices required to maintain and improve healthy forests.

Why are they important?

FRA 2015 indicators provide a picture of the current state of the world's forest resources and most importantly of the changes over the last 25-year period. All this information, made available by countries to FRA and the global community, constitutes a basis for the development of policies, practices and investments affecting forests and forestry.

Given the complexity of the worlds' forests and the societal benefits from forests, no single indicator can adequately assess progress towards sustainable forest management. The whole range of indicators must be considered to obtain a comprehensive picture.

What are the "future outlook" sections?

It is important to understand global forest resource dynamics from what has already occurred. It is also useful to take a look at what is likely to occur in coming years. At the end of each category of indicators there is a brief statement on what might be expected in the near future. These are based on trends seen in FRA 2015. The section of this document on looking to the future examines targets established by countries and a spatial model that explores future production and conservation forest changes. These are by nature speculative and are intended to stimulate thought, discussion and action.

ECOSYSTEM CONDITION AND PRODUCTIVITY

The extent and health of forest ecosystems is crucial in providing sustainable supplies of forest goods and services. Understanding changes in the forest resource is necessary for investment and management actions to sustain forests for future generations.

Changes in forest area

WHY IS THIS INDICATOR IMPORTANT?

Knowing how and why forest area changes over time is important for managing forests sustainably because such changes may result in long-term deletions (e.g. forest conversion to agriculture) from the forest land base or additions (e.g. afforestation). Because forests provide the bulk of the world's forest products and a number of ecological and environmental services, such as water purification, erosion control and carbon sequestration, it is vital to understand current forest resources and the many paths by which forests are changing. Forests also act as sinks and sources of carbon, so monitoring forest additions and deletions through land-use change helps scientists and decision-makers to gauge the forests' ability to reduce net greenhouse gas (GHG) emissions.

Changes in forest area often relate to changes in the ability of forest to provide globally important goods and services. These can include employment, wood products, non-wood forest products and services. Understanding these changes provides a sound basis for policy, investment and management decision-making at the national, regional and global scales.

WHAT HAS CHANGED AND WHY?

Over the past 25 years forest area has changed from 4.1 billion ha to just under 4 billion ha, a decrease of 3.1 percent. The rate of global forest area change has slowed by more than 50 percent between 1990 and 2015 (Table 1). This change results from a combination of reduced forest conversion rates in some countries and increased forest area expansion in others. It appears that net forest area change has stabilized over the past decade. This is an important development given the fact that wood removals in 2011 are about 200 million m³ higher per year than in 1990 and human populations have grown during this period by about 37 percent.

Annual forest change from 2010 to 2015 demonstrates positive change: a reduction in forest loss rates. Figure 1 shows how forest area as a proportion of land area is globally distributed as of 2015. The top ten forest

countries account for some 67 percent of global forest area (Table 2).

The ways in which this area has changed over the past 25 years is important, particularly given the continued growth in human populations and demand for forest products. Tables 3 and 4 show where the greatest changes occur in forest area.

By far the largest area of forest converted to other land uses between 1990 and 2015 was in the tropics, which has shown losses in every measurement period since 1990 (Figure 2). Net forest area has increased in temperate countries in every measurement period, while there has been relatively little change in the boreal and subtropical climatic domains.

The largest proportion of the world's forest is in high-income countries, followed by upper middle- lower middle- and low-income countries. This is true for total forest area, primary forest, other naturally regenerated and planted forest (Figure 3).

Figure 4 shows countries with stable forest area, and forest area gains and losses from 1990 to 2015.

While forest area has declined, human populations have increased, meaning that per capita forest area is declining – a trend that has existed for many millennia. Changes in per capita forest area are, like other measures of forest area change, uneven across climatic domains and subregions.

TABLE 1 **Global forest area change (1990–2015)**

Year	Forest (000 ha)	Annual change (000 ha)	Annualized[a] Change
1990	4 128 269		
2000	4 055 602	−7 267	−0.18
2005	4 032 743	−4 572	−0.11
2010	4 015 673	−3 414	−0.08
2015	3 999 134	−3 308	−0.08

[a] Calculated as the compound annual growth rate.

FIGURE 1   **Forest area as a percentage of total land area in 2015**

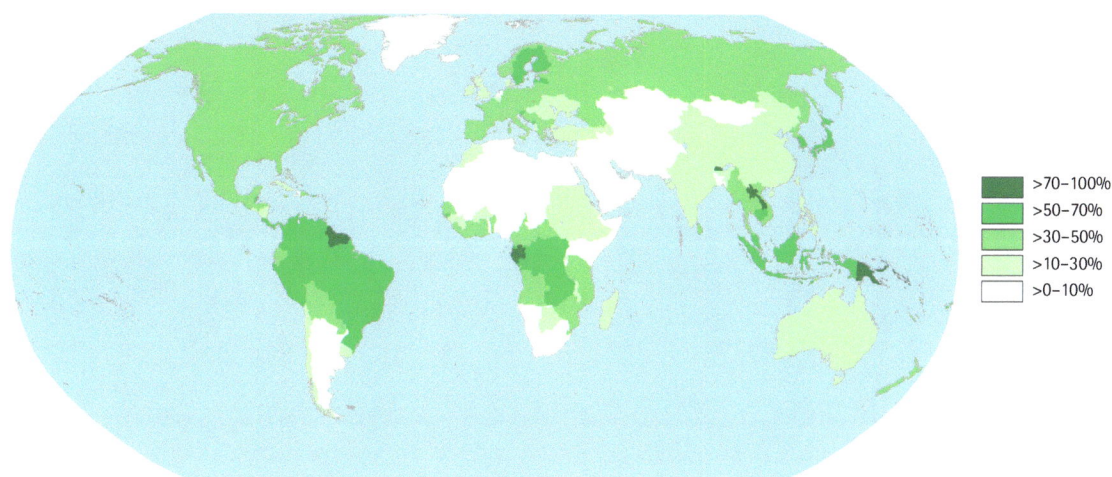

Legend:
- >70–100%
- >50–70%
- >30–50%
- >10–30%
- >0–10%

TABLE 2   **Top ten countries by forest area in 2015**

	Country	Forest area (000 ha)	% of country area	% global forest area
1	Russian Federation	814 931	48	20
2	Brazil	493 538	58	12
3	Canada	347 069	35	9
4	United States of America	310 095	32	8
5	China	208 321	22	5
6	Democratic Republic of the Congo	152 578	65	4
7	Australia	124 751	16	3
8	Indonesia	91 010	50	2
9	Peru	73 973	58	2
10	India	70 682	22	2
	Total	**2 686 948**		**67**

TABLE 3   **Countries reporting the greatest annual forest area reduction (2010–2015)**

	Country	Annual forest loss Area (000 ha)	% of 2010 forest area
1	Brazil	984	0.2
2	Indonesia	684	0.7
3	Myanmar	546	1.7
4	Nigeria	410	4.5
5	United Republic of Tanzania	372	0.8
6	Paraguay	325	1.9
7	Zimbabwe	312	2.0
8	Democratic Republic of the Congo	311	0.2
9	Argentina	297	1.0
10	Venezuela (Bolivarian Republic of)	289	0.5

TABLE 4   **Countries reporting the greatest annual forest area gain (2010–2015)**

	Country	Annual forest area gain Area (000 ha)	% of 2010 forest area
1	China	1 542	0.8
2	Australia	308	0.2
3	Chile	301	1.9
4	United States of America	275	0.1
5	Philippines	240	3.5
6	Gabon	200	0.9
7	Lao People's Democratic Republic	189	1.1
8	India	178	0.3
9	Viet Nam	129	0.9
10	France	113	0.7

FIGURE 2 **Annual forest area change by climatic domain (000 ha per year)**

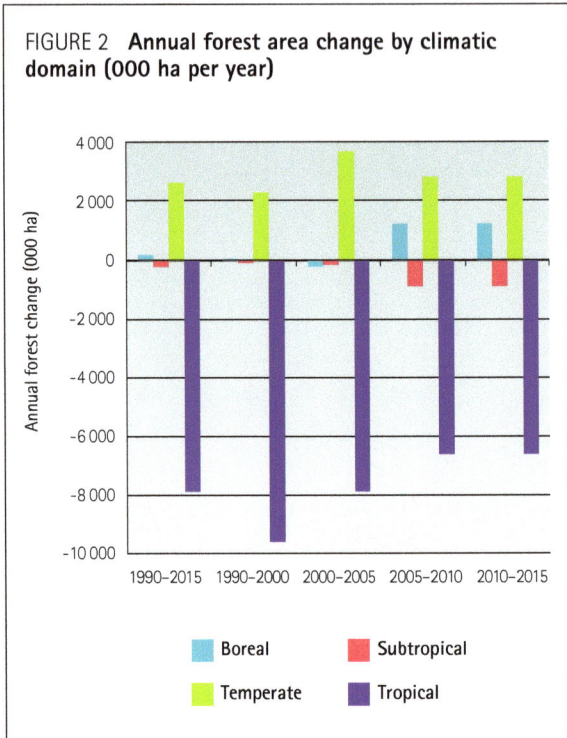

FIGURE 3 **Forest distribution by income category (2015)**

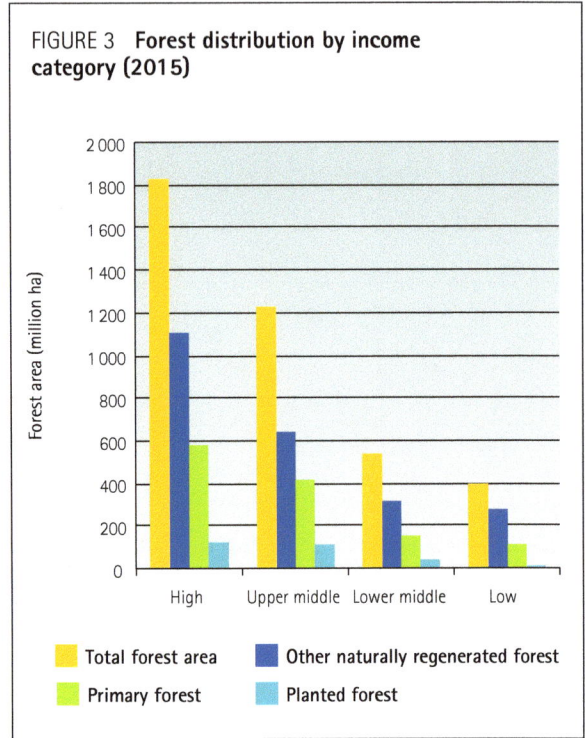

FIGURE 4 **Annual net forest gain/loss (ha) by country (1990–2015)**

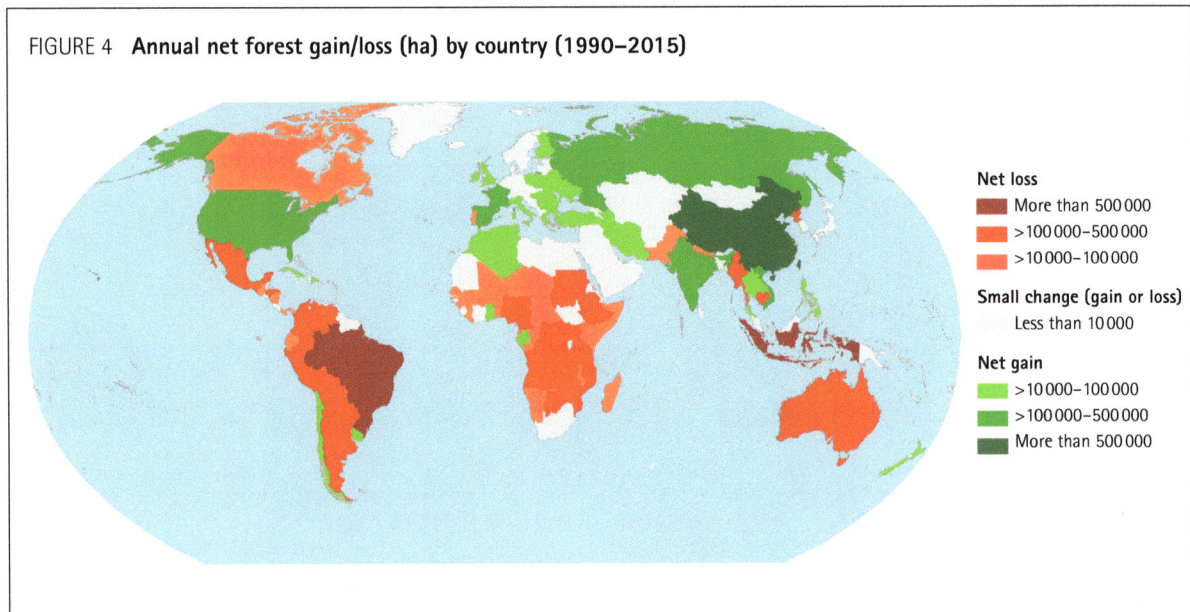

Forest land use vs tree cover: Why is this important?

FRA provides statistics on forest area as forest land use. This means that land reported as forest may not always have standing forest but is counted as forest as long as the intention is to re-vegetate the land as forest within five to ten years. Think of cropland: a maize field in the winter or long dry season is bare, yet it is still a maize field. The same applies to forest land. Other global estimates report tree canopy cover regardless of whether the trees are forest or horticultural species or whether the land has just been harvested prior to replanting. This results in inaccurate estimates of deforestation both in time and space.

Change in boreal and temperate domains has been gradual while decline in per capita forest in the tropics has not – per capita forest area has nearly halved over the last twenty-five years (Figure 5). In the subtropics it has declined by over 35 percent.

Forest area change among high-income countries has been positive over the last 25 years, with increases averaging over 0.05 percent per year. Upper middle-income countries have the second largest proportion of forest area and have managed to reduce annual forest loss from a rate of 0.14 percent from 1990 to 2000 to no appreciable change from 2010 to 2015.

Clearly, forest area gains and reductions in forest loss have been greatest in the high- and upper middle-income categories (Figure 6), while loss rates have remained virtually unchanged over the past 25 years in the low-income category. Forest change in lower middle-income countries has gone from 0.60 percent annual change to 0.35 percent change from 1990 to 2015, yet the rate of change appears to be stable and remains consistently negative. For low-income countries the rates of forest losses are essentially unchanged, with annual rates between 0.57 percent and 0.64 percent over the 25-year period.

WHAT IS THE FUTURE OUTLOOK?
The decrease in net forest loss rates in the tropics and subtropics, combined with stable or moderate increases in the temperate and boreal zones, suggests that the rate of forest loss will probably continue to decrease in coming years. As human populations continue to

increase, it is likely that demand will continue for conversion of more forest land to agriculture, particularly in the tropics (unless agricultural productivity increases substantially on existing agricultural lands). The decline in per capita forest area, coupled with steady increases in wood removals, indicates that more wood will be needed from less land in coming years.

Natural and planted forest area change

WHY IS THIS INDICATOR IMPORTANT?
The similarities and differences between natural and planted forests is a topic of debate among many stakeholders interested in forest change. Natural forests contribute to conserving the diversity of genotypes and maintaining the natural tree species composition, structure and ecological dynamics and often provide critical supplies of forest products. Planted forests are often established for the purpose of production, or wind erosion control and/or protection of soil and water. Well-managed planted forests can be useful in providing various forest goods and services and helping to reduce the pressure on natural forests.

WHAT HAS CHANGED AND WHY?
Globally, natural forest area is decreasing and planted forest area is increasing. As of 2015 natural forest accounts for 93 percent of total forest area with planted forest occupying 7 percent, or 290 million ha.

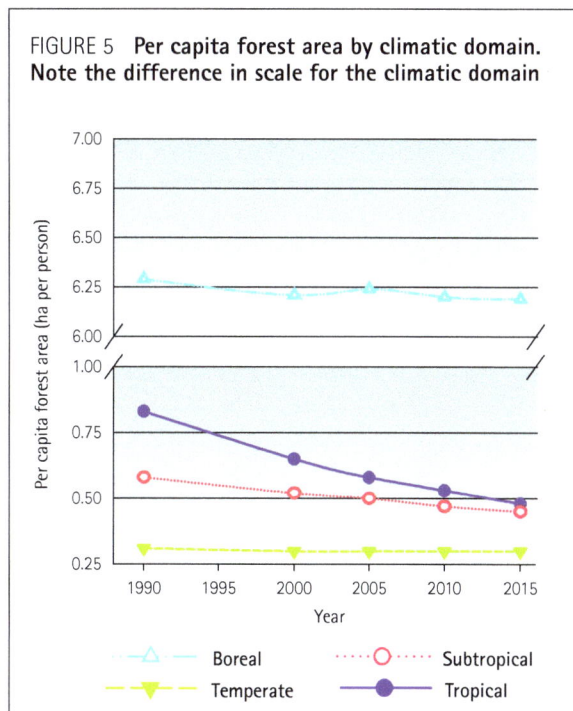

FIGURE 5   **Per capita forest area by climatic domain. Note the difference in scale for the climatic domain**

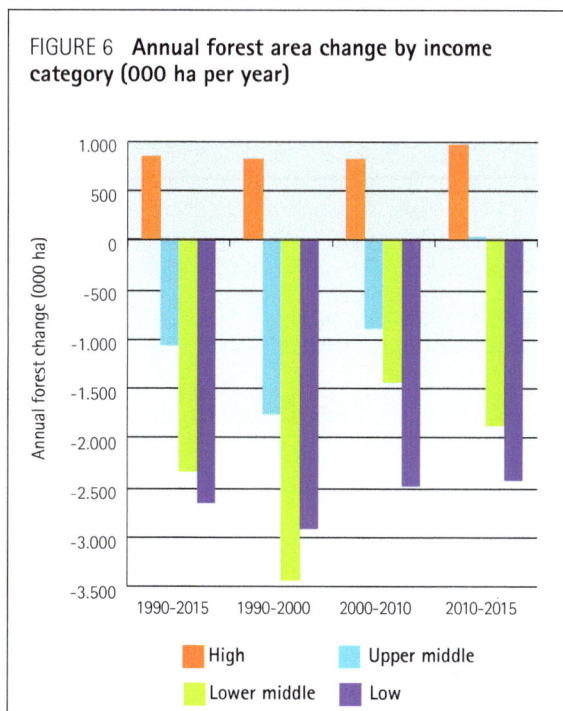

FIGURE 6   **Annual forest area change by income category (000 ha per year)**

The net loss of natural forest has decreased from some 8.5 million ha per year in the 1990s to a net of 6.6 million ha per year from 2010-2015. This comes from a loss of 8.8 million ha per year and a gain of 2.2 million ha per year. Gains come from natural forest area expansion, often on former agricultural lands.

The largest area of natural forest is found in Europe with about 900 million ha (Figure 7), of which about 88 percent is in the Russian Federation. South America accounted for the largest loss in natural forest. In this region, the area of natural forest decreased by an estimated 3.5 million ha per year between 1990 and 2000 and slowed down to 2.1 million ha per year between 2010 and 2015. A similar trend occurred across sub-Saharan Africa. East Asia reported the largest increase in natural forest area: about 450 000 ha per year since 1990. In Europe, Oceania and the Caribbean the trend is relatively stable.

Planted forest area increased by over 110 million ha since 1990 and accounts for 7 percent of the world's forest area. The average annual rate of increase between 1990 and 2000 was 3.6 million ha. The rate peaked at 5.2 million ha per year for the period 2000 to 2010 and slowed to 3.1 million ha (2010 to 2015) per year, as planting decreased in East Asia, Europe, North America, South Asia and Southeast Asia. During this period planted forests increased by a net of 3.1 million ha per year (3.5 million ha of planted forest gain minus 0.4 million ha of planted forest loss).

The largest area of planted forest is found in the temperate zone, accounting for 150 million ha, followed by the tropical and boreal zones with about 57 million ha each. Over the last 25 years the area of planted forest increased in all climatic domains, most notably in the boreal domain, where it almost doubled. In the tropical and temperate zones, it increased by 69 percent and 57 percent respectively (Figure 8).

Planted forest includes a wide range of productive, protective and multiple-use plantings for commercial and non-commercial use. They include both species mixtures and monocultures with a broad range of management intensity and purpose. They supply timber (including woodfuel), non-wood forest products and many of the environmental services provided by natural forests.

Trees outside forests

While not technically considered as forest according to the standard forest definition used by FAO and many other international organizations, trees outside forests are a valuable source of many products and services found in forests. In some countries they provide critical supplies of wood, fruits and other non-wood forest products. For FRA 2015 the area of trees outside forests was reported to be 284 million ha in 2015, which is an increase from the 274 million ha reported for 1990. This is partially due to a larger number of countries reporting (87 reported for 1990 whereas 98 reported for 2015). While substantially more difficult and costly to measure than forest at a national scale, it is clear that trees outside forests are a critical natural resource.

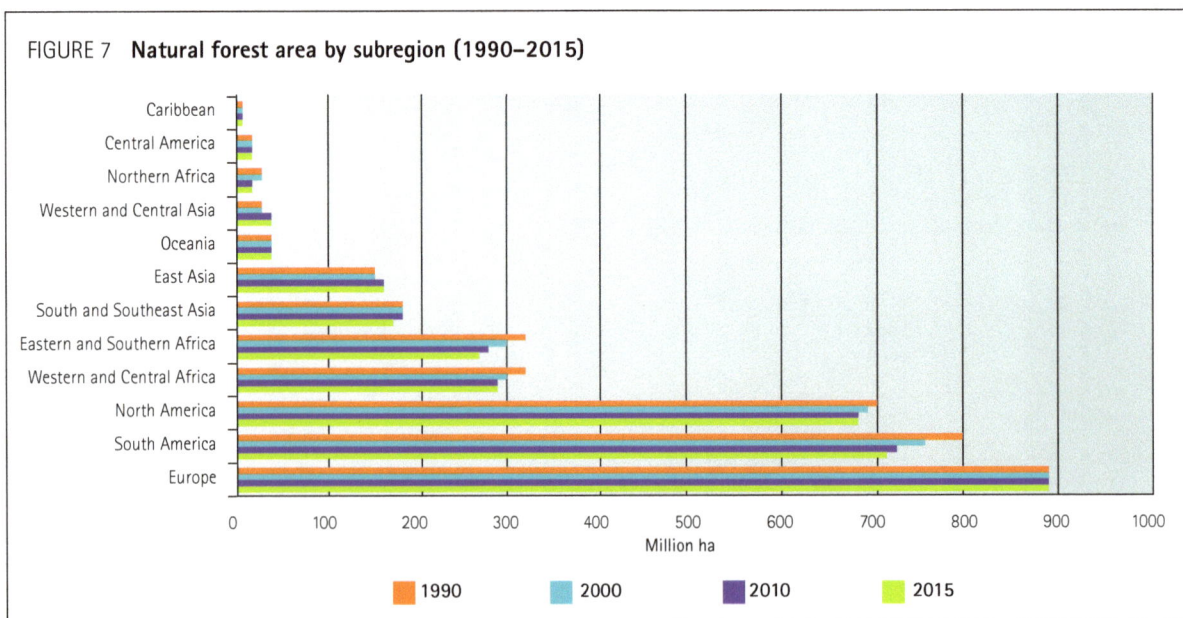

FIGURE 7   Natural forest area by subregion (1990–2015)

FIGURE 8   Planted forest area by climatic domain

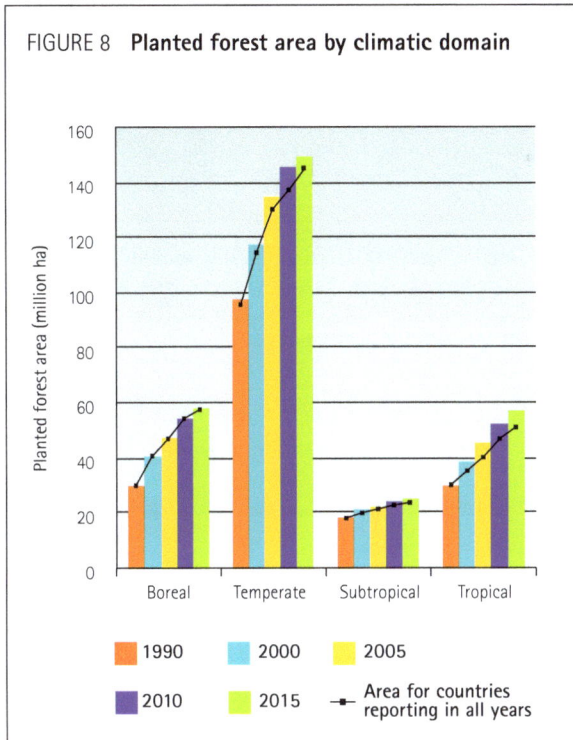

Planted forest area (million ha)

Legend:
- 1990
- 2000
- 2005
- 2010
- 2015
- ● Area for countries reporting in all years

Climatic domains: Boreal, Temperate, Subtropical, Tropical

WHAT IS THE FUTURE OUTLOOK?

Although the rate of decrease of natural forest has slowed down during the last ten years, natural forest area will probably continue to decline, particularly in the tropics, primarily due to conversion of forest to agriculture. On the other hand, due to a growing demand for forest products and environmental services, the area of planted forests is likely to continue to increase in coming years.

Partial canopy cover loss – a proxy for forest degradation?

WHY IS THIS INDICATOR IMPORTANT?

Forest degradation is a critical parameter to monitor for impacts on biodiversity, atmospheric carbon flux and as a precursor to potential forest conversion. Measuring forest degradation is problematic, however, for several reasons. First, forest degradation is notoriously difficult to define. Second, forest degradation, by any definition, is difficult to detect with most forms of measurement as it is a subtle form of forest change. Detecting degradation from remotely sensed data, especially with the most commonly used forms of medium spatial resolution data, is difficult because the scale at which the degradation takes place is often at sub-pixel resolution. This means that the nature of the degradation affects areas smaller than the detection capability of the remotely sensed pixel.

HOW WAS THIS DONE?

Time series from the Moderate Resolution Imaging Spectroradiometer satellite (MODIS) VCF data, with a pixel size of 250 m, have been analysed for indications of partial canopy removal. This involved calculating the slope of the line formed by the annual percentage tree-cover estimates and absolute range of percentage tree-cover measurements over time. As the pixel size is coarse, only areas with a relatively large amount of partial canopy cover removal can be detected. The global Intact Forest Landscapes and Global Wetland Map has been used for ancillary datasets to decrease the risk of false detections where partial canopy cover loss (PCCL) is unlikely. While PCCL may relate to forest degradation, it also includes areas that are under sustainable forest management.

WHAT HAS CHANGED AND WHY?

Partial canopy cover loss was summed for all years between 2000 and 2012, thus there is no time series of estimates to determine what has changed with its rates or locations. The total area of PCCL was 185 million ha but is unevenly spread across climatic domains (Figure 9). The tropical climatic domain had the most PCCL detected, on over 156 million ha, or 9 percent of the domain. Both the boreal and subtropical climatic domains indicated approximately 2 percent PCCL (1.8 percent and 2.1 percent, respectively). The area of PCCL was greater than forest gain only in the boreal domain (by three times); in all other domains forest loss or gain was larger than the area of PCCL (Figure 9).

©FAO/Francisco Miguel Agostinho

Figure 10 presents results for PCCL by subregion. Forest loss was greater than the area of PCCL in Eastern and Southern Africa (almost four times), South America (almost double) and Central America. South and Southeast Asia exhibited the largest amount of PCCL, with over 50 million ha detected. Results for South America indicated approximately 47 million ha. Western and Central Africa was third with approximately 35 million ha of PCCL. Expressed as a proportion of total forest area in 2010, the subregion with the largest amount of PCCL was Central America with approximately 18 percent of the forest area indicated as PCCL.

WHAT IS THE FUTURE OUTLOOK?

Additional forest canopy cover loss will certainly occur, from selective harvesting, maintenance of lower stocking densities, fire, pest, disease and/or livestock grazing. Evidence of weather shifts as a result of climate change seems to suggest that some species will be affected more than others, so that in mixed stands additional gaps will emerge over time. These gaps may eventually be filled by other species. Changes in PCCL will also reflect natural processes of known cyclic episodes of insect and disease outbreak. Causes of PCCL include not only those anthropogenic actions which may be considered harmful to the functioning of intact forests, but also human management activity and natural causes which are part

of properly functioning forest ecosystems or could be considered enhancements to forest systems. Thus, large areas of PCCL are probably caused by fire, whereas others are considered to be under sustainable forest management regimes.

FIGURE 9 **Total PCCL estimates aggregated by climatic zone (orange bars) compared with net forest loss 2000-2010 from Country Reports (blue bars): negative values indicate net forest gain**

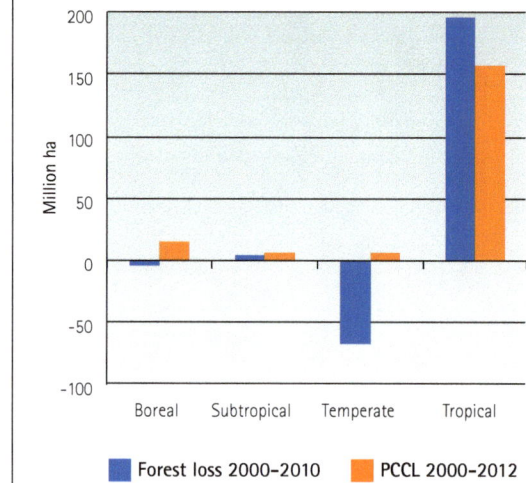

FIGURE 10 **Total PCCL estimates aggregated by FRA subregion (orange bars) compared with net forest loss (2000-2010) from Country Reports (blue bars): negative values indicate net forest gain**

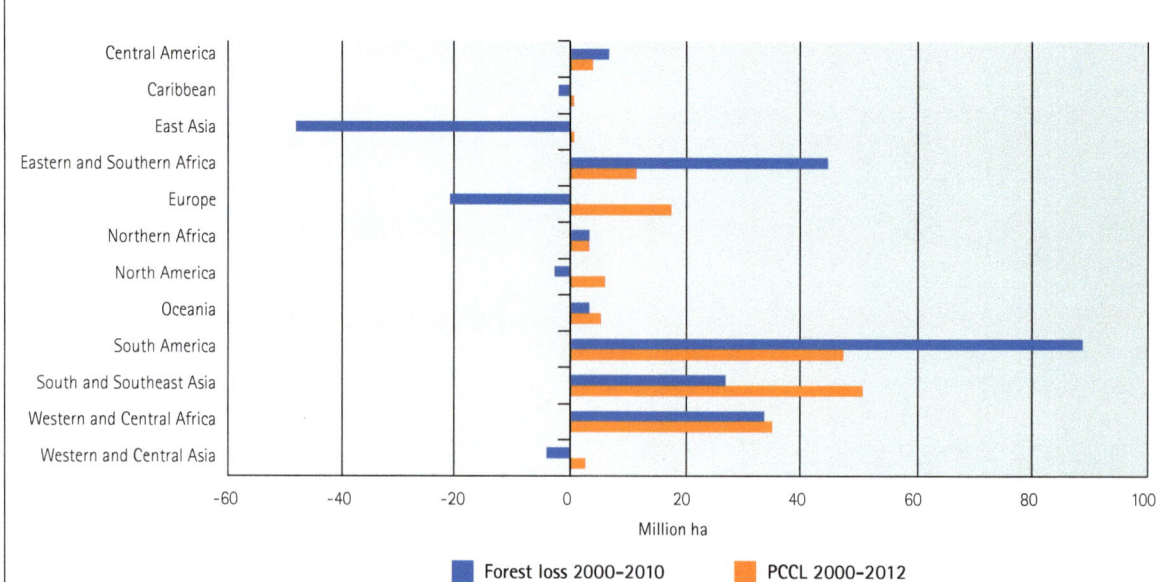

SUSTAINABLE FOREST MANAGEMENT

Sustainable forest management means different things to different people. It includes the use of social, environmental and economic criteria that help to maintain the flow of forest goods and services without significant degradation over time.[4] Essentially it is forest management for the long term: the production of forest goods and services to meet the needs of present and future generations while preserving natural capital.

WHY IS THIS SET OF INDICATORS IMPORTANT?

Sustainable forest management (SFM) is encouraged by the presence of enabling conditions. These conditions include the national legal, policy and institutional frameworks. With an unfavourable governance system, long-term management involves risks and uncertainties that may be too high for investors in sustainable forest management. This includes investments by governments and the private sector, non-governmental organizations, donors, individuals and communities. Enabling practices that encourage SFM make these investments more attractive.

WHAT HAS CHANGED AND WHY?

A number of key indicators suggest substantial progress towards SFM in recent years. These changes can be summarized as follows:

- Legal frameworks, stakeholder inputs, data availability, national inventories and management plans cover about 1.1 billion ha of forest land.

- Permanent forest increased slightly between 1990 and 2015.

- Area covered by forest management plans has increased over time, split evenly between production and conservation.

- On average, forest management plan (FMP) monitoring takes place every three years in the tropics.

- High conservation value forests (HCVF) and social considerations are in almost all FMPs; soil and water management considerations are less common.

- Certification increased in almost all climatic domains from 2000 to 2014, with the greatest increases in the high-income/temperate zone. A total of 438 million ha is under international forest management certification.

- Forest area inventoried increased dramatically in the last five years, 85 percent of that in the high- and upper middle-income countries. In 2014, 112 countries reported having forest inventories that cover some 3 242 million ha or approximately 82 percent of the world's forests. Almost all (96 percent) forest inventories used ground plots and about 70 percent of all national forest inventories use an integrated approach of aerial or satellite imagery in combination with ground-based measurements.

Using the SFM indicators collected through FRA 2015, we can begin with the area of permanent forest[5] and evaluate how much forest land is covered by successive indicators. Figure 11 presents such a framework and begins from the left, showing the forest area where conditions encourage SFM. Moving left to right, Figure 11 shows the total area of forest designated as permanent forest land and the areas of the permanent forest that are subject to each of the "SFM tools" listed on the horizontal axis. This area is reduced based on the extent of supportive legal frameworks, data availability, management planning and stakeholder involvement in operations. It demonstrates that almost all countries with permanent forest have policies, laws and regulations that support SFM; about 98 percent of global permanent forest area is covered by policies or regulations that support SFM. This indicates a broad intention by governments to support SFM into the future on around 2.2 billion ha (55 percent of global forest area in 2015). With all the SFM tools included, the area decreases to 1.1 billion ha globally (50 percent of permanent forest area).

---

[4] The United Nations definition of SFM is "[a] dynamic and evolving concept [that] aims to maintain and enhance the economic, social and environmental values of all types of forests, for the benefit of present and future generations". United Nations General Assembly resolution A/RES/62/98, 31 January 2008.

[5] A combination of legally defined permanent forest (i.e. the permanent forest estate) and government estimates of private forest land that are highly likely to remain in permanent forest use.

FIGURE 11   **The area of permanent forest use as modified by other elements of the SFM enabling environment: (A) permanent forest use; (B) SFM policies; (C) SFM legislation; (D) stakeholder platform; (E) forest inventory; (F) national reporting; (G) forest management plans; (H–J) soil and water conservation, high conservation value forest and social engagement as part of forest management plans; (K–M) stakeholder involvement in operational planning, operations and review**

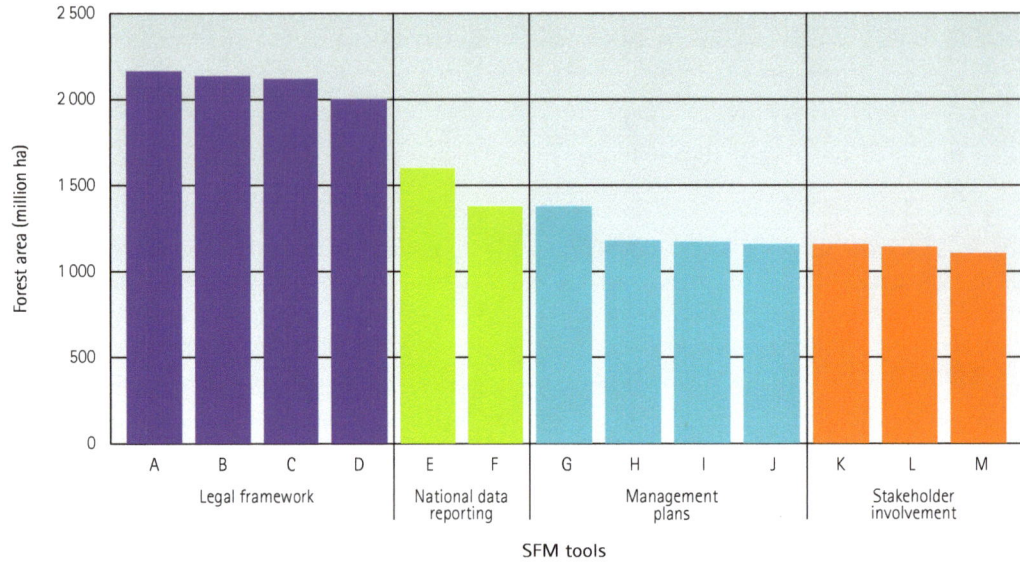

How much forest is intended to be kept in the long term?

WHY IS THIS INDICATOR IMPORTANT?

Most forests are owned by governments or private individuals or companies. Within government ownership there are forest lands that are by law or regulation mandated to remain as forest. The FRA report calls these lands the permanent forest estate. Private owners (who owned some 19 percent of total forest area in 2010) may not be required by law to retain their holdings as forest *in perpetuity*, yet many private owners also have this intent. For some types of private ownership there are legal instruments designed to maintain permanent forest. This indicator captures both public (permanent forest estate) and private holdings expected to remain in permanent forest land use.

Not all forest land that exists today will exist into the future. Having an indication of how much land is presently regarded as permanent forest provides insights into accumulated government and private plans for retaining forest in permanent use, and the need to develop policies that encourage the establishment of new forests. China is a good example of how interest in increasing the permanent forest estate has led to large-scale afforestation from both natural expansion (regeneration) and planting.

WHAT HAS CHANGED?

In 1990 the area declared permanent forest estate was 1.4 billion ha (FRA 2010) or 34 percent of the total forest area; by 2010 this proportion had risen to 37 percent (FRA 2015). However, the total amount of forest land intended to be permanently in forest was 54 percent of total forest area in 2010 (Figure 12). The difference between these

FIGURE 12   **Permanent forest lands compared with total forest area (2010)**

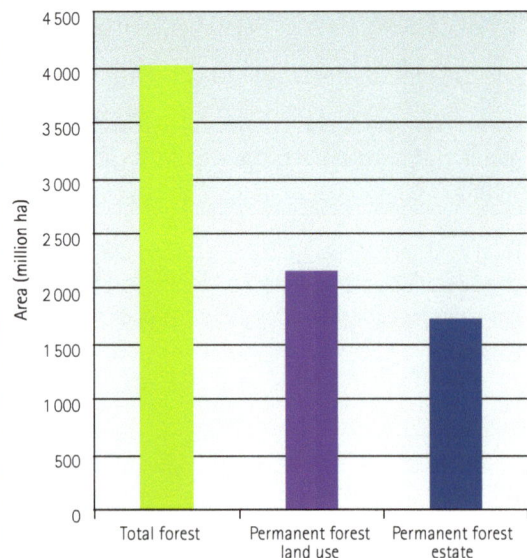

two numbers comes from the addition of private forest lands intended to remain in forest to state-mandated permanent forest estate.

The proportion of permanent forest that is mandated by the state (PFE) also varies across income categories (Figure 13). In low-income countries the amount of permanent forest is much less than in other categories, while that mandated by the state accounts for almost the entire permanent forest land category. The lower middle-income category has the highest proportion of private land in the permanent category (43 percent) while the high-income category has the largest forest land area contribution from privately owned forest land.

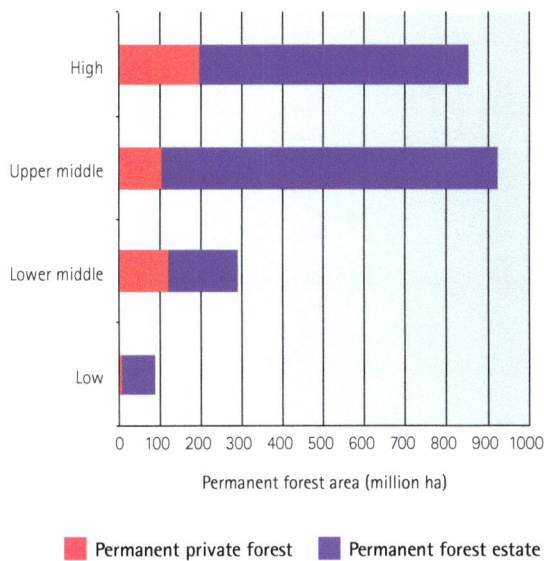

FIGURE 13 **Permanent forest land by income category and type (2010)**

Permanent forest area (million ha)

■ Permanent private forest   ■ Permanent forest estate

Forest management plans

WHY IS THIS INDICATOR IMPORTANT?
The sustained supply of forest goods and services is best achieved through long-term investment and forest management planning. This often means that management responsibilities for any particular forest will pass over time among individuals, companies and government agencies. To ensure forests are managed with the long term in mind, management plans are used for production, conservation, and environmental services.

WHAT HAS CHANGED?
The proportion of forest area covered by management plans varies dramatically across subregions. Central America, Europe and South Asia report very high proportions (>80 percent) of total forest while Africa, Oceania and South America report low proportions (<30 percent) (Figure 14). The boreal zone has the greatest proportion covered by forest management plans (FMPs) and the tropical climatic domain has the lowest (Table 5).

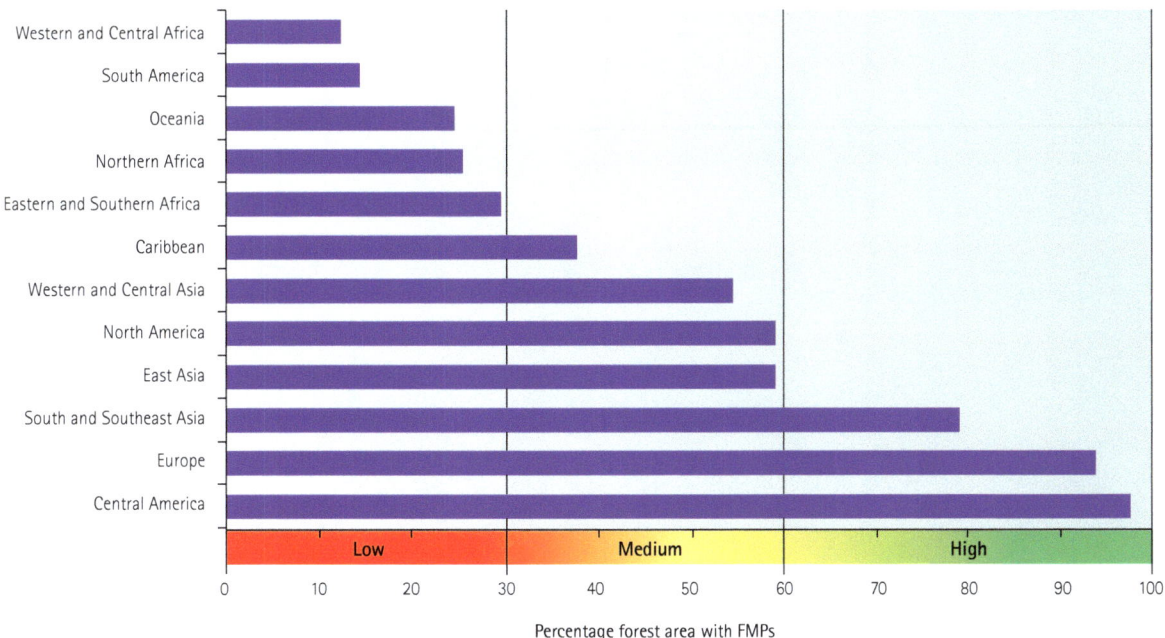

FIGURE 14 **Proportion of forest area covered by forest management plans by subregion (2010)**

Percentage forest area with FMPs

In 1953, only 27 percent of the world's production forests were covered by management plans. In 2010, 70 percent of production forest had management plans. The total area under management plans in 2010 was 2 100 million ha or 52 percent of the total forest area. A significant change since the 1950s is that management plans in 2010 were evenly split in area between production and conservation purposes, the two being almost equal at global level (Table 5).

Forest management plans are in some cases not implemented due to lack of compliance enforcement. Frequency of monitoring is reported to be quite high, with the most frequent monitoring reported in tropical countries. Over 35 percent of management plans in the

tropics are monitored every year, resulting – in theory at least – in the monitoring of every management plan every three years.

Globally, forest management plans contain several common elements relating to protection and community involvement (Figure 15). Soil and water management and the delineation of high conservation value forests are required in forest management plans on over 60 percent and 80 percent of global forest area, respectively. This suggests a formal recognition of the importance of environmental requirements in managed forests. Social considerations and community involvement are likewise required for management planning on over 80 percent of global forest area.

TABLE 5 **Forest area with forest management plan by climatic domain**

Domain	Forest with FMP		FMP for production		FMP for conservation	
	Area (000 ha)	% of domain forest area	Area (000 ha)	% of domain forest area	Area (000 ha)	% of domain forest area
Tropical	509 761	28.2	191 267	10.6	203 787	11.3
Temperate	424 971	63.1	175 516	26.1	209 428	31.1
Boreal	1 073 801	87.7	442 734	36.1	401 497	32.8
Boreal without Russian Federation	258 656	63.1	21 243	5.2	7 852	1.9
Subtropical	91 131	28.5	36 505	11.4	28 678	8.9
Total	**2 099 664**		**846 021**		**843 391**	

FIGURE 15 **Percentage of forest area with management plans that include soil and water management, high conservation value forest delineation and social considerations**

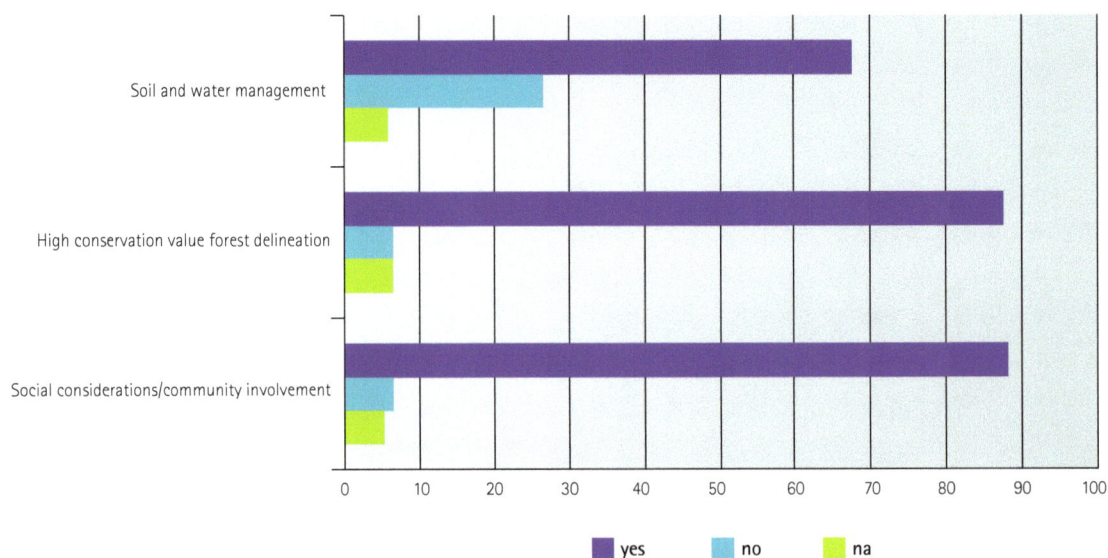

Forest management certification

WHY IS THIS INDICATOR IMPORTANT?

Interest in maintaining and enhancing forest attributes and indicators of long-term sustainability has led to broad interest in sustainable forest management. While the interest is wide-ranging, agreement on what this means is not. Many of the principles are accepted but the specifics are often seen differently by different stakeholders. Forest management certification includes the definition of forest management practices that meet requirements for best practice in areas including: biodiversity, sustainable production of goods and environmental services, minimal chemical use, protection of workers' rights and welfare, local employment, respect for indigenous peoples' rights and forest operations undertaken within the national legal framework following best practices.

Forest management certification is not a perfect tool for describing sustainable forest management. However, it is an important proxy that can be monitored and verified independently to a known standard. Certification with third-party verification provides a good indication that the forest manager is investing in continuous improvement to ensure the use of best practices that will result in stable forest production and conservation values. Certification may be the best single means of evaluating progress towards sustainable forest management, as it is relatively easy to document.

WHAT HAS CHANGED AND WHY?

The area covered by forest management certification has grown dramatically from 18 million ha in 2000 to over 430 million ha in 2014, an increase of over twentyfold. However, the expectation was that certification would be most helpful in the tropics where practices are perceived as less sustainable than in other climatic domains. Yet the most rapid, sustained growth in international certification continues to be in the temperate and boreal zones (Figure 16).[6]

While growth has been relatively constant for both of the major certification schemes, it has declined for reported domestic certification schemes. This is primarily due to changes in reporting for the major domestic schemes in North America and does not yet adequately reflect the emergence of domestic schemes in Indonesia and elsewhere.

Forest monitoring and reporting

WHY IS THIS INDICATOR IMPORTANT?

National forest reporting provides a means of communicating with specialists and the public about forest characteristics and change. Detecting and understanding forest resource change depends entirely on continuous

---

[6] Does not account for possible double counting due to multiple certifications, which is approximately 2 percent of the total, mostly in Europe (see Fernholz and Kraxner, 2012, pp. 107–116).

FIGURE 16 A AND B **Area of international forest management certification (2000–2014): (A) Forest Stewardship Council (FSC); (B) Programme for Endorsement of Forest Certification (PEFC)**

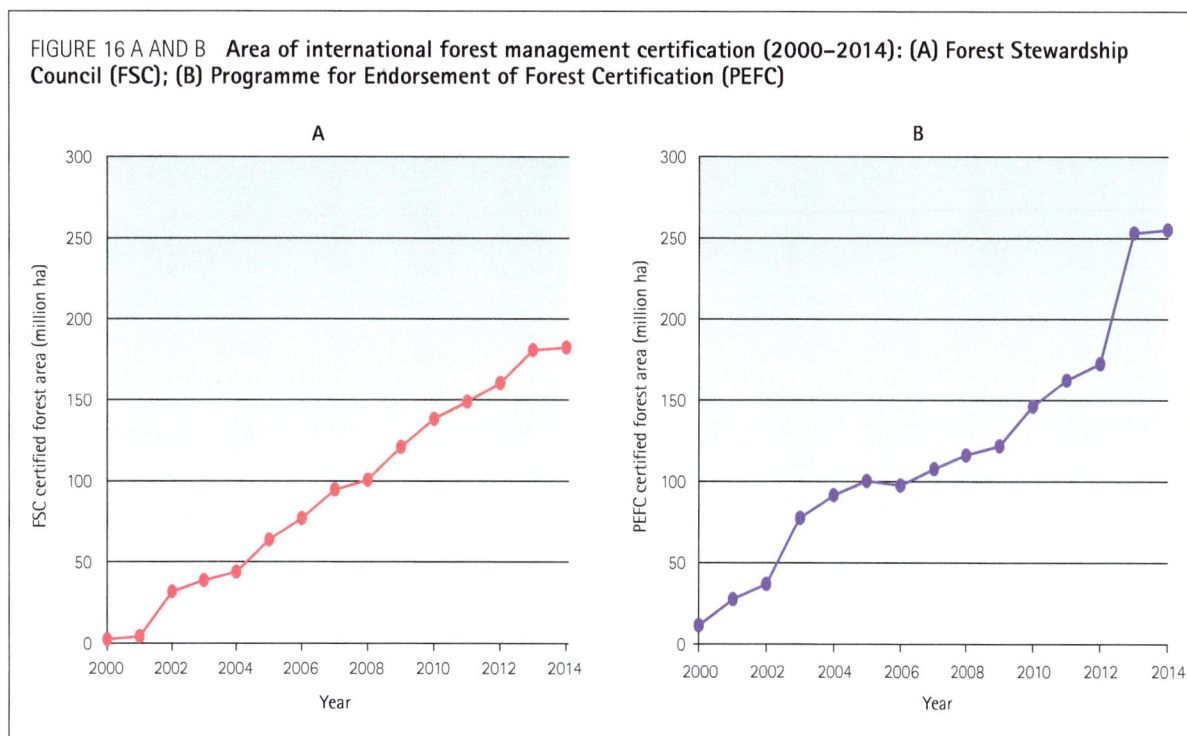

or repeated forest inventory and monitoring activities. Without monitoring, the nature and direction of forest change would be based on guesswork. Forest monitoring is the foundation of forest management and investment in forests and forestry by governments, private companies, international donors, individuals and civil society.

WHAT HAS CHANGED AND WHY?

There has been a remarkable increase in the forest area covered by recent or ongoing national inventories. Some 81 percent of the world's forest area was covered by forest inventories with the most recent measurements made between 2011 and 2015 (Figure 17). For only about 13 percent of global forest area were the most recent inventory measurements made before 2011. By 2015, 112 countries had recently conducted or are implementing forest inventories that in total cover over 3 billion ha of forest land.

In addition, these countries reported a high proportion of continuous or repeated forest inventory programmes

(almost 94 percent) although an undetermined number of these countries do not have specific plans for repeated measurements. Compared with an inventory conducted only once, repeated inventories enhance precision and confidence of the estimates and provide forest change estimates.

From an analysis at the climatic domain level, inventory activities have been carried out on only 61 percent of forest area of the tropical domain, compared with the higher proportion of forest area inventoried in the other domains: 100 percent for boreal, 98 percent for subtropical and 95 percent for temperate domains.

There is a very strong relationship between wealth (or income categories) and the amount of forest area inventoried (Table 6). High-income countries reported national inventories covering almost all of the forest area (98 percent) within the group, 28 of the 55 upper middle-income category countries reported 80 percent coverage, 25 of the 48 lower middle-income reported 55 percent coverage and 17 of the 33 low-income countries reported 37 percent coverage within this grouping.

Countries have made significant commitments to report on their forests, with about 92 percent of global forest area covered by at least one type of public reporting. No reports were produced by 38 nations that represent just 5 percent of the global forest area.

Although all national reporting is important, periodic national "state of the forest" reports can be particularly helpful by providing fundamental reference levels for determining forest changes over time. There are 116 countries that report on almost 90 percent of the global forest area through this kind of report. Even better are Criteria and Indicators (C&I) reports, which can provide the greatest insight into that country's progress towards SFM, as they are designed to provide comprehensive information on social, economic and environmental aspects. C&I reports were drafted by 86 countries, covering 77 percent of global forest area. Nearly all of the forest area not covered by C&I reports is in the low income category countries (Figure 18).

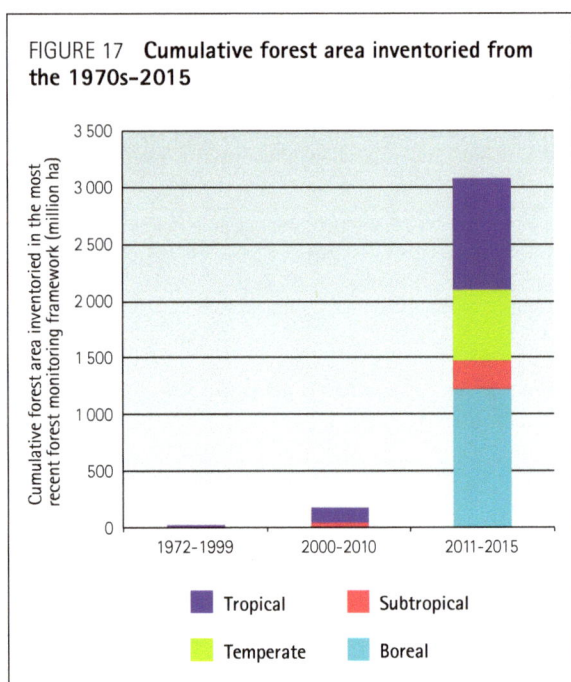

FIGURE 17   Cumulative forest area inventoried from the 1970s–2015

TABLE 6   Income grouping and national forest inventory

Income category	% of forest area with inventory by income group	Area with inventory (000)	Total area of forest for income group (000)
High	98	1 807 621	1 830 480
Upper middle	80	985 556	1 224 998
Lower middle	55	290 440	532 705
Low	37	146 809	398 135

FIGURE 18 Distribution of forest area not covered by C&I reports

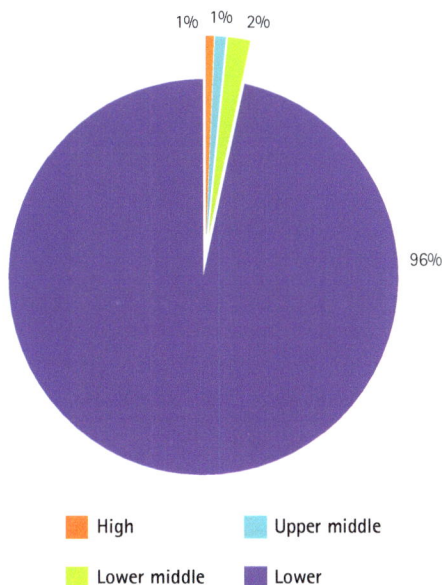

1%   1%   2%

96%

■ High   ■ Upper middle
■ Lower middle ■ Lower

Permanent forest estate area as a proportion of total forest has increased slightly due to the reduction in total forest but there has been little change in the area of PFE. This stability in the area designated by the state as permanent forest estate over a 25-year period provides a good indication that the 1.5 billion ha designation will persist into the foreseeable future. Less certain is whether the amount of private forest land is likely to remain forest, even though the percentage of forest owned privately at the global scale is increasing.

The proportion of forest area covered by management plans seems likely to either remain stable or increase, with a growing interest in effective monitoring and enabling of plan revisions as management needs change. As the area of forest management certification increases, the area covered by FMPs that are monitored independently also increases. As solid information on existing forest resources improves through forest inventory, the basis for good management planning also expands.

The dramatic rise in forest inventory coverage in recent years indicates an increasing number of countries involved in national forest inventories. We can reasonably expect this trend to continue. With the potential for REDD+[7] payments based on performance, there are additional incentives to conduct inventories for many countries in the tropics.

In addition, the high proportion of countries conducting continuous or repeated forest inventory programmes offers optimism for the steady improvement of future forest resource information.

WHAT IS THE FUTURE OUTLOOK?

It is reasonable to expect that, ultimately, virtually all forest countries will have SFM-supportive policies and regulations. The challenge will be to construct regulations so that forest managers are encouraged to follow them, by making investments in practical improvements profitable over a reasonable period. Support of SFM at the legal, data, management planning and stakeholder involvement levels is critical in facilitating long-term forest management. This applies to governments, private companies, communities and individuals.

---

[7] Reducing Emissions from Deforestation and Forest Degradation.

MAINTAINING ECOLOGICAL INTEGRITY AND BIODIVERSITY

Forests play an important role in supporting and maintaining ecological systems and cycles. Forests both depend on and contribute to the many complex processes that are responsible for recycling carbon and water. They also regulate water flows and protect soils. How forests are managed can affect their future roles in maintaining genetic and taxonomic variation, ecosystem functions and environmental services.

Conservation and protected areas

WHY IS THIS INDICATOR IMPORTANT?
Maintenance of biodiversity through conservation and protected areas allows species to survive, evolve and dynamically adapt to changing environmental conditions. It also enhances plant and animal gene pools and provides genetic reservoirs for tree breeding. Conserving biodiversity is thus crucial for the long-term health and sustainable productivity of the world's forests. Reliable data on forest biological diversity provides an indication of countries where biodiversity may be increasing or decreasing.

The area of primary forest, forest primarily designated for the conservation of biodiversity and forests within legally established protected areas[8] were analysed to monitor changes in forest biodiversity over time.

WHAT HAS CHANGED AND WHY?
In 2015 primary forest accounted for 33 percent of the world's forest, or about 1.3 billion ha; half of that is located in the tropics. At the regional level the largest extent of primary forest is found in South America, followed by North and Central America. Over half of the world's primary forest is found in only three countries: Brazil, Canada and the Russian Federation. Information on the state of primary forest in 2015 was available for 203 countries and territories, representing 97 percent of the global forest area. Still, many countries relied on proxies, such as the extent of forest within national parks and conservation areas, to estimate the extent of primary forest.

Primary forest area change should be viewed with some caution, particularly for the tropics. Only 33 percent of the primary forest area reported was classified as Tier 3 (the highest quality category) and 57 percent was Tier 1, which is the least reliable category. It is difficult for most

countries to delineate primary forest, particularly when the definition is strictly applied. Increases generally come from reclassifications at the national scale; for example, the designation of new wilderness or protected areas of untouched forest.

At the climatic domain level, the total area of primary forest appears to have increased or remained stable from 1990 to 2015 for all domains (Figure 19). However, for the tropics part of this is due to an increase in the number of countries reporting over time (111 in 1990, and 119 in 2015) and not necessarily an increase in primary forest. The Figure 19 line for countries reporting in all years is comparable with the total primary forest area reported for all domains except the tropics, where there has been a loss of primary forest in countries that reported every year. Primary forest area increased throughout the reporting period in high-income countries, and decreased in low-income countries.

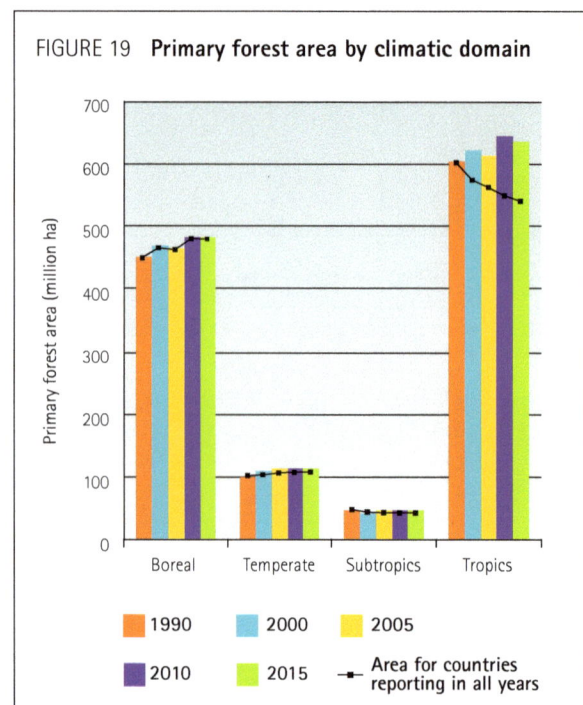

FIGURE 19 **Primary forest area by climatic domain**

---

[8] For the terms and definitions of FRA 2015 variables, see *FRA 2015 Terms and Definitions* (available at http://www.fao.org/docrep/017/ap862e/ap862e00.pdf).

FIGURE 20 **Selected countries that reported a negative annual change in primary forest area and a positive annual change in other naturally regenerated forest area (1990–2015)**

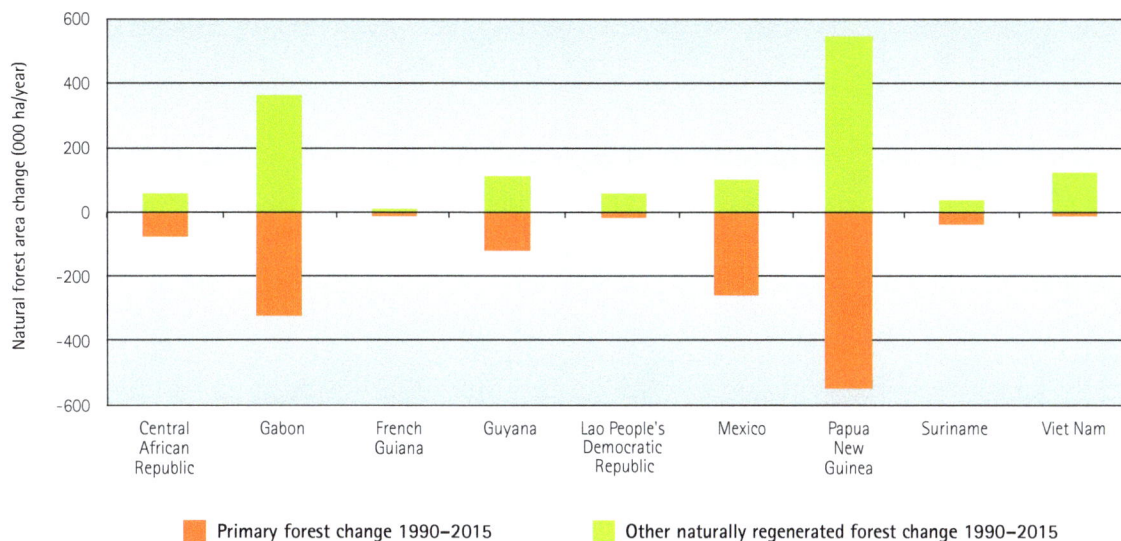

TABLE 7 **Top ten countries for forest area designated primarily for conservation of biological diversity in 2015**

	Country	Forest area designated primarily for conservation of biological diversity (000 ha)	% of country forest area reported
1	United States of America	64 763	21
2	Brazil	46 969	10
3	Mexico	28 049	42
4	Russian Federation	26 511	3
5	Australia	26 397	21
6	Democratic Republic of the Congo	26 314	17
7	Venezuela (Bolivarian Republic of)	24 313	52
8	Canada	23 924	7
9	Indonesia	21 233	23
10	Peru	19 674	27
	Total	**308 147**	

Information is still emerging on what proportion of the decrease in primary forest area is due to deforestation and what is due to reclassification to other forest types, as a result of forest management operations or other human interventions. A comparison of annual change over time of primary and other naturally regenerated forest highlighted that among the countries that reported a decrease in primary forest over the last 25 years, 13 countries (representing 54 percent of the total primary forest loss) reported an increase in the area of naturally regenerated forest (Figure 20). For some of these countries the correspondence between lost primary forest and increase in naturally regenerated forest is particularly evident, suggesting that the loss of primary forest could be mainly due to conversion to other natural forests.

In other countries (for example, Brazil) that show decreases in both "other naturally regenerated forest" and primary forest, and a slight increase in planted forest, it is more difficult to formulate hypotheses about primary forest dynamics.

Forest area primarily designated for biodiversity conservation accounts for 13 percent of the world's forest, or 524 million ha, with the largest areas reported in Brazil and the United States of America (Table 7). The area of forest designated for that purpose has increased by 150 million ha since 1990 but the rate of annual increase slowed down during the last five years. Over the last five-year period, Africa reported the highest annual increase in the area of conservation forest. Europe, North and Central America and South America reported the lowest, compared with previous reporting periods. The annual increase reported by Asia for 2010–2015

TABLE 8 **Top ten countries for forest area within protected areas in 2015**

	Country	Forest area within protected areas (000 ha)	% of country forest area reported
1	Brazil	206 227	42
2	United States of America	32 863	11
3	Indonesia	32 211	35
4	China	28 097	13
5	Democratic Republic of the Congo	24 297	16
6	Venezuela (Bolivarian Republic of)	24 046	52
7	Canada	23 924	7
8	Australia	21 422	17
9	Peru	18 844	25
10	Russian Federation	17 667	2
	Total	**429 598**	

FIGURE 21 **Forest in protected areas by climatic domain**

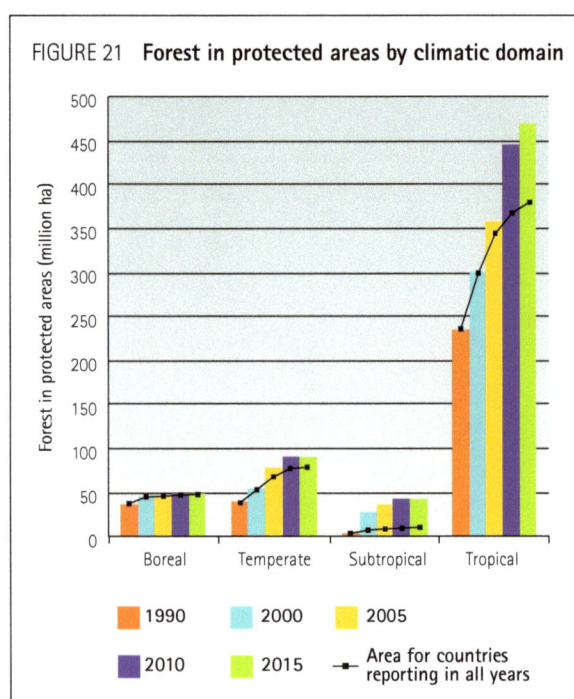

was lower than that reported for 2000–2010 but higher than the increase reported in the 1990s.

Seventeen percent of the world's forests are located within legally established protected areas, accounting for 651 million ha. South America reported the highest percentage (34 percent) of protected forest. That was mainly due to Brazil where 42 percent of the forests are located within the protected areas network (Table 8). The area of forest within protected areas has increased by 210 million ha since 1990 but the rate of increase slowed during the period 2010–2015. The increase in the area of forest within protected areas was particularly evident in the tropics, where an additional 144 million ha of new forests have been put under protection since 1990 (Figure 21).

WHAT IS THE FUTURE OUTLOOK?
Deforestation, forest degradation and fragmentation, pollution and climate change are all having negative impacts on forest biodiversity. The analysis confirmed that despite mounting conservation efforts over the past 25 years, the threat of biodiversity loss, reflected in the degradation or loss of primary forest, persists and is likely to continue. Possible future trends are not easy to delineate due to the reliability of data and lack of more detailed information on primary forest dynamics. Although more areas of forest will probably be designated for biodiversity conservation, tangible results in reducing biodiversity loss will be achieved only through integration of conservation policies into broader national and local development programmes and through more systematic consideration of trade-offs between biodiversity conservation and other needs of society. The expansion of sustainable forest management practices will also enhance biodiversity conservation.

Biomass and carbon stock changes

WHY IS THIS INDICATOR IMPORTANT?
The biomass and carbon stocks in forests are important indicators of forests' productive capacities, energy potential, and capacity to sequester carbon. The role of forests as terrestrial sinks and sources of carbon dioxide has received increasing attention since the adoption of the 1997 Kyoto Protocol to the United Nations Framework Convention on Climate Change (UNFCCC).

FIGURE 22 **Changes in carbon stocks in forest biomass 1990–2015 (million metric tonnes C per year)**

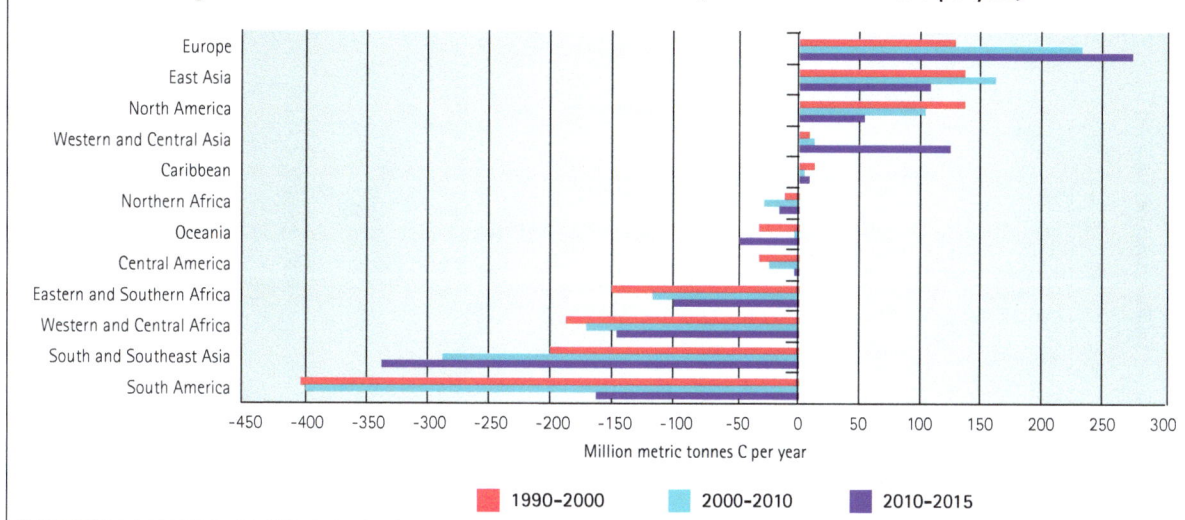

WHAT HAS CHANGED AND WHY?

The world's forests store an estimated 296 Gt of carbon[9] in both above- and below-ground biomass, which contains almost half of the total carbon stored in forests. The highest densities of carbon are found in forests of South America and Western and Central Africa, storing about 120 tonnes of carbon per hectare in the living biomass alone. The global average is close to 75 tonnes per hectare.

Over the past 25 years the carbon stocks in forest biomass decreased by almost 17.4 Gt, equivalent to a reduction of 697 million tonnes per year or about 2.5 Gt of carbon dioxide (CO_2). The reduction is mainly driven by carbon stock changes as a result of converting forest lands to agriculture and settlements and degradation of forest land. Africa, South and Southeast Asia and South America account for most of the losses (Figure 22). Carbon stocks increased most in East Asia, Europe, North America, and Western and Central Asia. Caribbean reported only a slight increase.

Over the 25-year period net losses decreased from 1.2 Gt per year in the 1990s to 0.4 Gt per year between 2000 and 2010 and 0.2 Gt per year between 2010 and 2015. One reason for the change is the effect of countries in South and Central America and Asia that have managed to significantly slow the rate of loss. Brazil alone reported that the annual loss of carbon in above- and below-ground biomass was reduced from 193 million tonnes of carbon per year in the 1990s to about 63 million tonnes per year for 2010–2015.

WHAT IS THE FUTURE OUTLOOK?

The current global trend of decreasing carbon stocks is likely to continue but losses can eventually be expected to level out. The application of REDD+ and other initiatives has

contributed to increased awareness of the role that forests have as terrestrial sinks and sources of carbon dioxide. New data will probably continue to show changes in the quantities of greenhouse gas emissions from forests. The use of woody biomass is likely to increase, as is the recognition that forests and forestry may reduce CO_2 emissions in other ways, such as through increased use of wood-based biofuels as a substitute for fossil fuels. Improved use of low energy-demanding construction materials such as wood and bamboo will continue to contribute to reductions of greenhouse gas emissions in substitution for high energy-intense materials such as iron and concrete. Harvested wood products can also play a role in carbon storage, providing greenhouse gas sequestration benefits.

Protection of soil, water and environmental services

WHY IS THIS INDICATOR IMPORTANT?

Forests deliver protection or conservation of natural resources, including soil and water, and other environmental services. Forests slow water dispersion and favour infiltration and percolation of rainwater, which recharges soil and underground water storage. This is crucial in supplying clean water for drinking, agriculture and other uses. Forests can protect soils from wind and water erosion, avalanches and landslides.

Forests provide habitats that support biodiversity and ecological processes and have cultural, religious and recreational values that are important to many forest users. Knowing whether or not these functions exist or are threatened helps governments to identify priority needs for restoration.

---

[9] This value includes both country reported values and estimates to fill data gaps.

FIGURE 23 **Change in global area allocated for (A) soil and water protection (based on 119 countries that reported this variable in all years) and (B) provision of environmental services for each forest climatic domain (based on 72 countries that reported this variable in all years)**

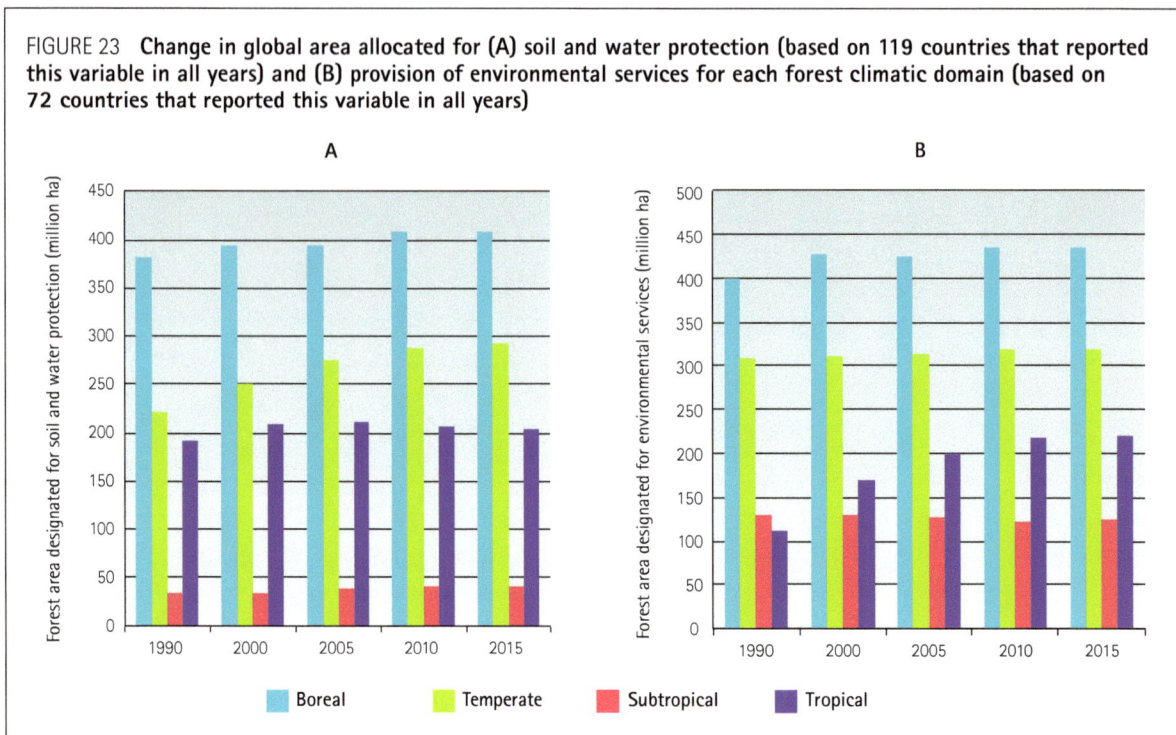

WHAT HAS CHANGED?

Countries reported increases of 185 million ha for soil and water conservation and 210 million ha for environmental services protection from 1990 to 2015. The area reported for soil and water protective functions increased by 5 percent in the last 25 years and a little more than 6 percent for environmental services. The geographic distribution of where these functions are reported shows relative changes between 1990 and 2015 (Figure 23). Most of Latin America and much of Africa, South Asia and Oceania reported little or no soil and water protective functions, even though they certainly exist in many forests in these regions. Notable is the relative lack of change between periods: most countries that reported in 2015 had reported similar proportions in 1990.

WHAT IS THE FUTURE OUTLOOK?

The forest area designated for protective functions is generally stable and is expected to remain so in the near future. There is increasing awareness of the importance of retaining these functions on both production and conservation of forest lands and the number of countries reporting is likely to increase. Given the current interest in forest land restoration, it is highly probable that more countries will also evaluate more forest area for the presence or absence of these functions and take steps to ameliorate forest degradation.

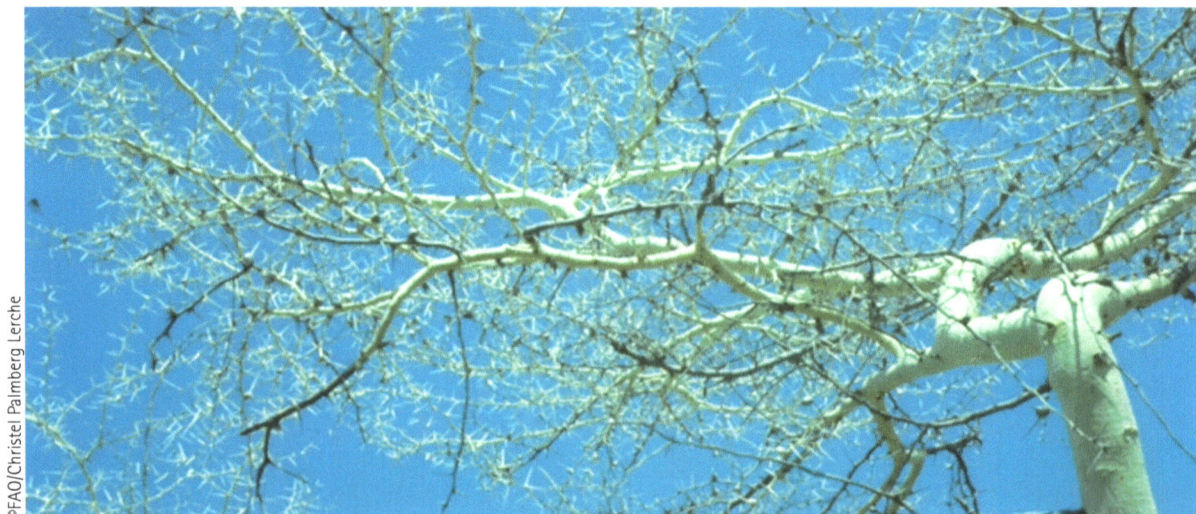

ECONOMIC AND SOCIAL BENEFITS

Sustainable forest management means ensuring that forests provide a broad range of goods and services over the long term, including significant economic and social benefits.

Trends in production, multiple-use forests and wood removals

WHY ARE THESE INDICATORS IMPORTANT?

Wood is part of almost everyone's life, whether in their use of paper or other wood products. The tracking of reported industrial roundwood and woodfuel removals provides an approximation of how much wood from the forest goes to meet these needs and how this demand changes. Most of the world's wood comes from production and multiple-use forest areas. For some countries this tracking also shows where wood removals are not significant in production or multiple-use forest and where trees outside forests or from other wooded land are more important. Analysis of trends in wood demand and the types of forest that supply timber and woodfuel help to highlight the importance of these forest classifications for long-term security of wood supplies.

WHAT HAS CHANGED AND WHY?

The demand for wood and the amount of forest land designated to produce it have increased since 1990. Wood demand has gone from 2.75 billion m³ per year in 1990 to 3.0 billion m³ per year in 2011. For the period 1990–2015, the area designated for wood production and multiple use increased by over 128 million ha.

Close to 1.2 billion ha of forests are designated for production, with more than half of this area found in high-income countries and only 8 percent in low-income countries (Figure 24A). There has been an increase of 47 million ha in reported production forest area since 1990. In addition, about 1 billion ha of forests are designated for multiple use, in most cases including the production of wood and non-wood forest products (Figure 24B). About two-thirds of the total forest area designated for multiple use are found in the high-income countries and only one tenth in the low-income countries. In the last 25-year period the area designated for multiple use has increased

FIGURE 24 **Forest area designated for (A) production (1990–2015) and (B) multiple use by income categories (1990–2015)**

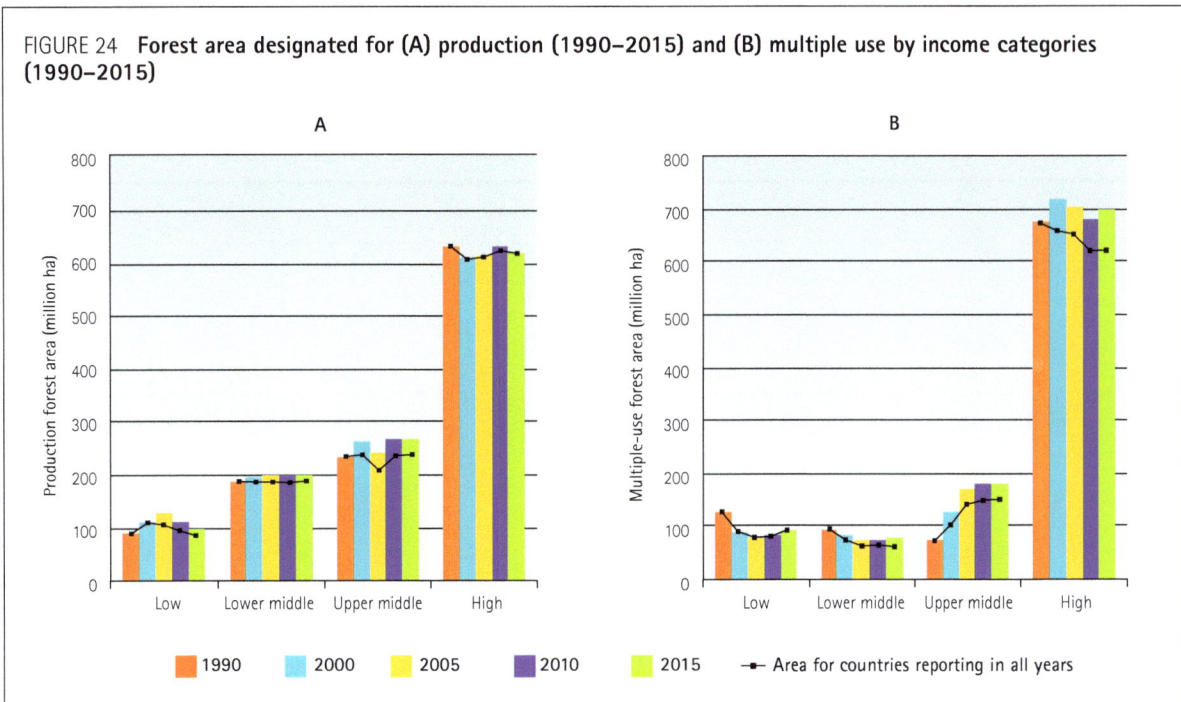

FIGURE 25 **Annual wood removals by income category**

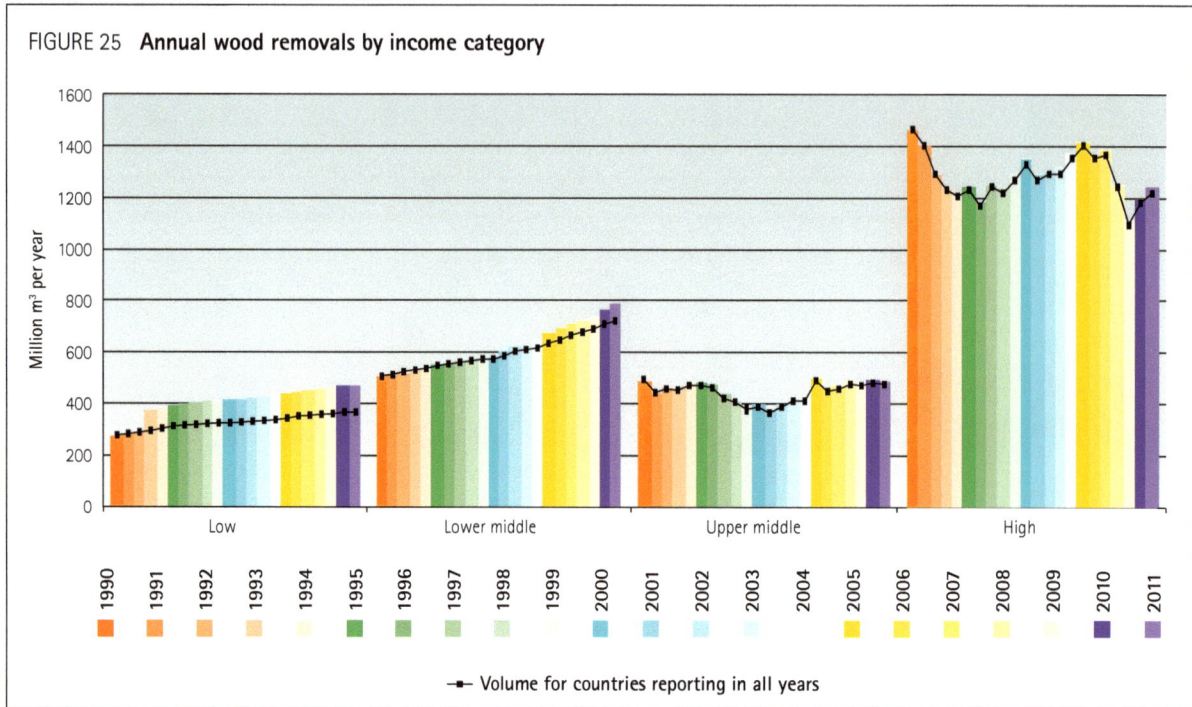

FIGURE 26 **Annual wood removals 1990–2011**

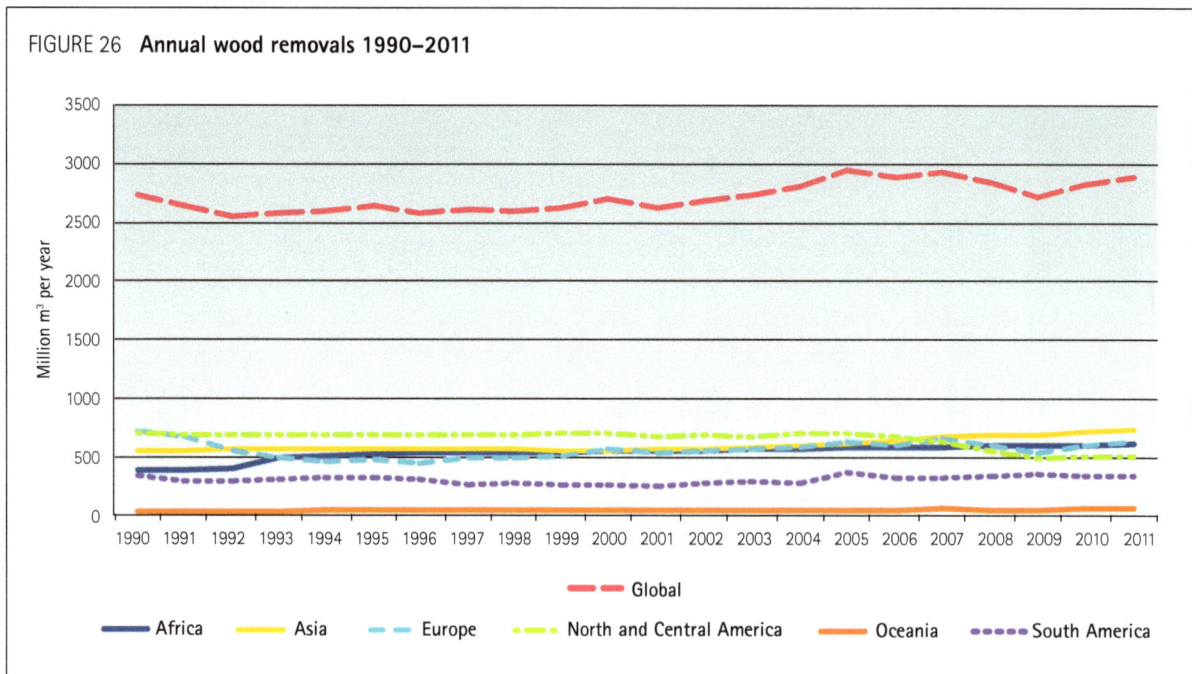

by some 82 million ha; most of this increase is in the upper middle-income countries (Figure 25).[10]

In 2011 global wood removals accounted for about 3 billion m³, equivalent to 0.65 percent of the total growing stock (Figure 26). Between 1990 and 2011 annual reported wood removals increased by some

250 million m³.[11] The lowest amount of wood removals was reported in 1992 (2.6 billion m³) mainly due to a sharp decrease reported by the Russian Federation. The highest amount of wood removals was observed in 2005 (almost 3 billion m³). Following the financial crisis of

---

[10] Note that this is based on the sum of all countries. The trend for countries reporting in all years can be seen in the line in Figure 24.

[11] This value uses the sum of all countries in both years. Missing data for 1990 are roughly estimated to be approximately 4 percent of the total wood removal volume for 1990 but are not included given the associated uncertainties.

2007–2008, Europe and North America together reported a decrease in wood removals from 1.3 billion m³ in 2007 down to 1 billion in 2009. This was followed by an increase to 1.1 billion in 2011 (Figure 26). Other regions did not indicate any significant reduction in total wood removals caused by the financial crisis. Countries with the highest wood removals are noted in Table 9.

Globally almost half of total removals are woodfuel but the share of woodfuel varies significantly by income category (Figure 27). For high-income countries the share of woodfuel is about 17 percent, for upper middle-income it is 41 percent, while in lower middle- and low-income countries it is 86 percent and 94 percent respectively. The highest share of forests

TABLE 9 **Top ten countries by wood removals in 2011**

	Country	Wood removals (2011) (1 000 m³ᵃ)	Woodfuel as % of total wood removals (2011)
1	India	434 766	88.6
2	United States of America	324 433	12.5
3	Brazil	228 929	50.7
4	Russian Federation	197 000	22.2
5	Canada	149 855	2.5
6	Ethiopia	104 209	97.2
7	Democratic Republic of the Congo	81 184	94.4
8	China	74 496	9.3
9	Nigeria	72 633	87
10	Sweden	72 103	8.2
	Total	**1 739 608**	

ᵃ Under bark

FIGURE 27 **Average industrial roundwood and woodfuel removals by income category (2009–2011)**

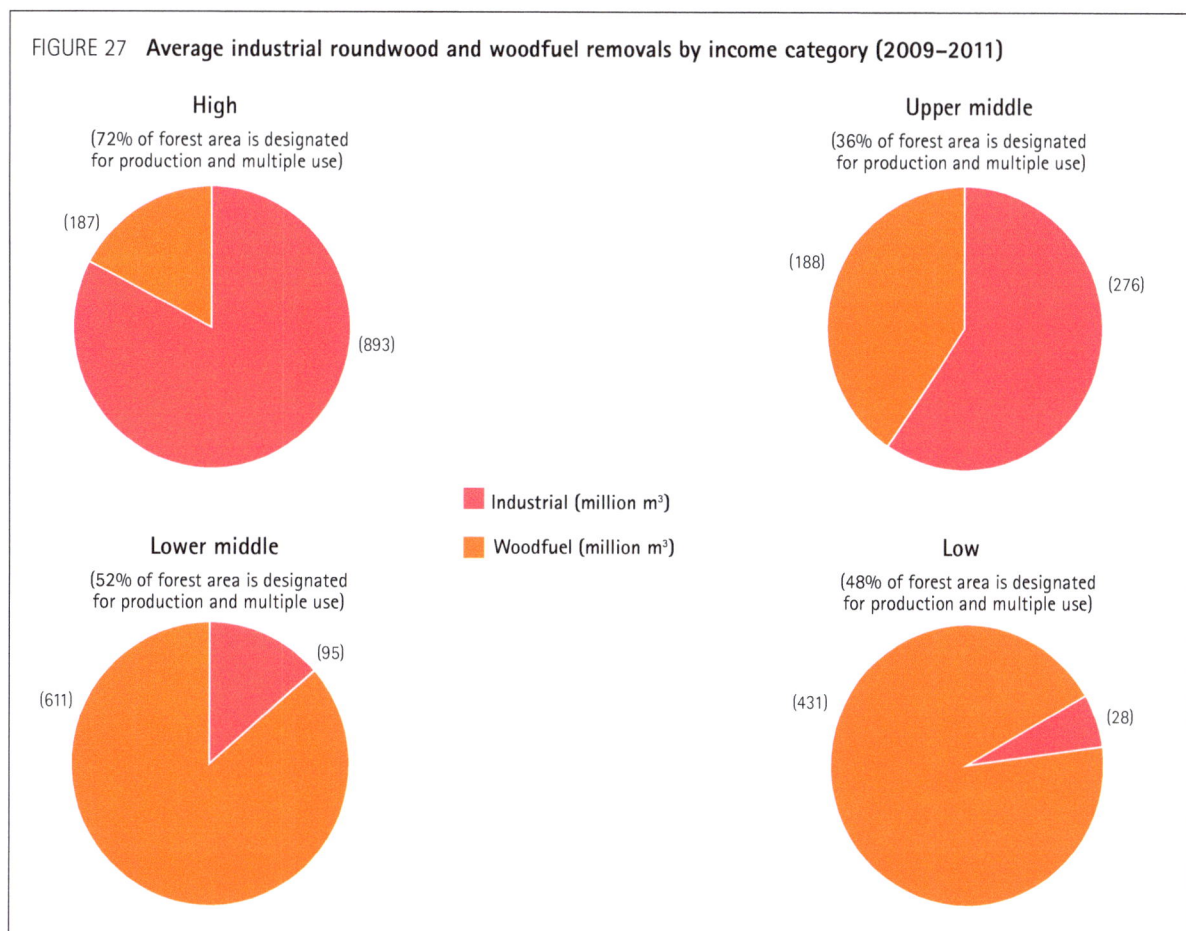

High
(72% of forest area is designated for production and multiple use)
(187)
(893)

Upper middle
(36% of forest area is designated for production and multiple use)
(188)
(276)

Industrial (million m³)
Woodfuel (million m³)

Lower middle
(52% of forest area is designated for production and multiple use)
(95)
(611)

Low
(48% of forest area is designated for production and multiple use)
(431)
(28)

designated for production and multiple use is found in high-income countries (72 percent), followed by lower middle- (52 percent), low- (48 percent) and upper middle- (36 percent) income countries.

WHAT IS THE FUTURE OUTLOOK?

Demand for wood products is likely to continue to increase globally. In high-income countries the share of woodfuel will probably increase as wood is a climate-friendly, renewable energy source, part of which will come from mill residues and lower-quality wood. In low-income countries the share will most likely decrease in most regions. Production and multiple-use forest area will probably remain stable, although it is also clear that a large proportion of wood removals will come from other wooded land, trees outside forests and forests designated for other purposes.

Contribution of forestry to gross domestic product

FRA has worked to harmonize procedures with the International Standard Industrial Classification of All Economic Activities (ISIC, 2008) since 2010. Following the ISIC, the boundaries of the forest sector can be summarized as the addition of three categories: *forestry and logging* (ISIC Rev. 4 Division 02), *wood industry* (ISIC Rev. 4 Division 16) and the *pulp and paper industry* (ISIC Rev. 4 Division 17). FRA 2015 is restricted to the primary production in the sector,

i.e. the category *forestry and logging* (ISIC Rev. 4 Division 02). Therefore the statistics of gross value added from forestry and the statistics on employment denote only activities within the category *forestry and logging*.

WHY IS THIS INDICATOR IMPORTANT?

Forestry contributes to a country's GDP in both formal and informal economic sectors. In many countries with rapidly expanding economies, the relative role of forestry and logging is decreasing at the national level. Yet the economic impact of revenue from forestry and logging is often felt most at the local level. Changes in the contributions of the within-forest activities reported in FRA 2015 reflect its economic importance at the national level. The value added is weighted by the total size of the economy; therefore this indicator reflects the performance of forestry, logging and GDP.

WHAT HAS CHANGED AND WHY?

The forest sector contributes about USD600 billion annually to global GDP, or about 0.8 percent of global GDP. Of this, forestry and logging in 2011 contributed some USD150 billion, which accounted for about 0.2 percent of the global economy. Globally, low-income countries accounted for only 4 percent of the global total value added from forestry and logging – however these contributions were often vitally important. High-income countries on average had the largest proportion of their forest land designated for production or multiple use and the lowest proportion of GDP from forestry; almost all of this value (84 percent) comes from timber rather than woodfuel (Figure 28).

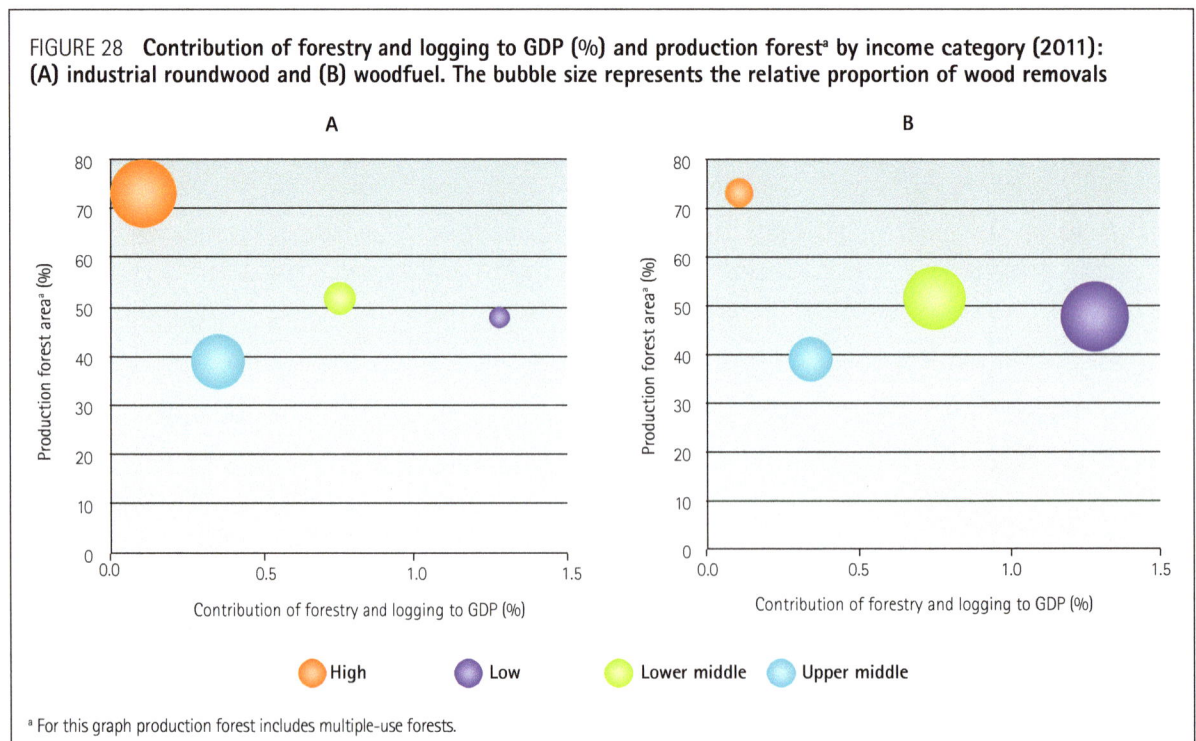

FIGURE 28 **Contribution of forestry and logging to GDP (%) and production forest[a] by income category (2011): (A) industrial roundwood and (B) woodfuel. The bubble size represents the relative proportion of wood removals**

[a] For this graph production forest includes multiple-use forests.

©FAO/K. MacDicken

Conversely, low-income countries have a smaller proportion of forest used for production and multiple use and most of the production is for woodfuel, yet forestry provides a much higher proportion of GDP (1.3 percent).

WHAT IS THE FUTURE OUTLOOK?
As national incomes increase, dependence on woodfuel for domestic use is likely to continue to decrease as a proportion of GDP. For low- and lower middle-income countries woodfuel contributions to GDP will remain important for the foreseeable future. For high-income countries, the value of the non-forest sector is likely to increase faster than the value added from forestry. However, in all cases value added from forestry is less important at the national scale than it is in local economies where communities and regions can be highly dependent upon forest-related income.

Non-wood forest products

Non-wood forest products (NWFPs) are often important sources of livelihood for rural dwellers and for industries that process or use these products. Understanding the value of NWFPs helps to highlight their importance in national economies and forest management strategies. Value in FRA 2015 is defined as the commercial market value at the forest gate.

TABLE 10 **Commercial value of NWFP removals in 2010 by income group category**

Income category	Million USD
Low	678
Lower middle	2 785
Upper middle	11 206
High	5 937
Total	**20 607**

Despite their importance, it is difficult to obtain reliable and consistent data on NWFPs, largely due to the fact that globally most NWFPs do not enter the commercial marketplace and data on non-commercial values are generally unreliable or totally absent. Data on the commercial value of NWFP removals is certainly a substantial underestimate of the value of NWFPs.

Employment in forestry

FRA 2015 includes data on full-time equivalent labour in forestry and logging. This is only labour in the forest, not the whole forest sector (which includes manufacturing and related employment). These values include both formal and informal employment estimates (ISIC/NACE Rev. 4 activity A02). This data complements those published in the *State of the World's Forests* report (FAO, 2014), which was assembled from a broad range of data sources.

WHY IS THIS INDICATOR IMPORTANT?
Employment in forestry and logging contributes to society's economic, environmental and social welfare. Forestry activities are carried out in rural areas where there are often few alternative sources of employment. That makes employment in these communities exceptionally important. Measuring and reporting employment provides an indication of how many rural jobs exist in forested areas.

WHAT HAS CHANGED AND WHY?
Employment in the forest in 2010 was around 12.7 million people (full-time equivalent), 79 percent of which was in Asia, mainly India, Bangladesh and China. Employment in forestry and logging remained relatively stable in the subtropical and boreal climatic domains and decreased in the temperate zone (Figure 29). There was an increase from 1990 to 2010 in employment in tropical countries, partly due to the low level of mechanization. Employment in the forest (mainly harvesting and silvicultural operations, including woodfuel and NWFP collection) is considered heavily under-reported due to a lack of data, particularly for informal or part-time employment.

Only 29 countries reported both employment and female employment for all years, showing that most countries do not have data disaggregated by gender. For those that report in all years the percentage of female employment has steadily increased from 20 percent in 1990 to 30 percent in 2010.

Countries with the highest number of women working in the forest were Bangladesh (600 000), China (301 000) and Mali (180 000). Countries with the greatest share of female employment were Mali (90 percent), Mongolia and Namibia (45 percent) and Bangladesh (40 percent). Bangladesh has updated its forest policy and legislation to enhance women's participation in social forestry development. In Mongolia, women have historically been responsible for such forestry activities as woodfuel collecting, reforestation and education, while in Mali women are actively involved in woodfuel and NWFP collection.

FIGURE 29   **Changes in forest employment (1990–2010)**

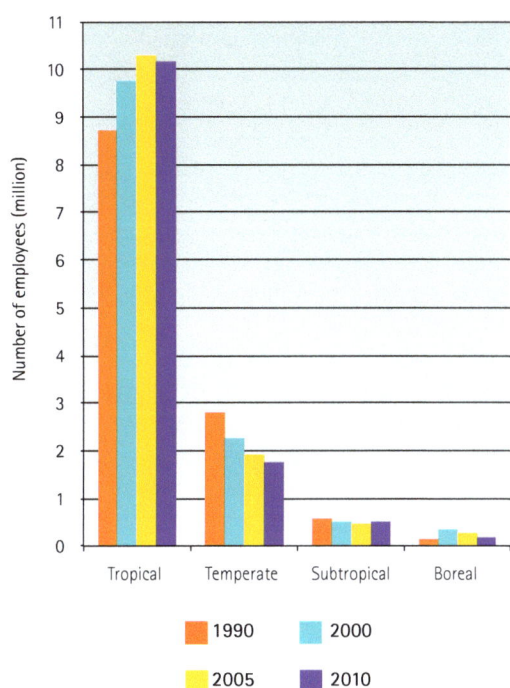

FIGURE 30   **Productivity per domain (2000–2010)**

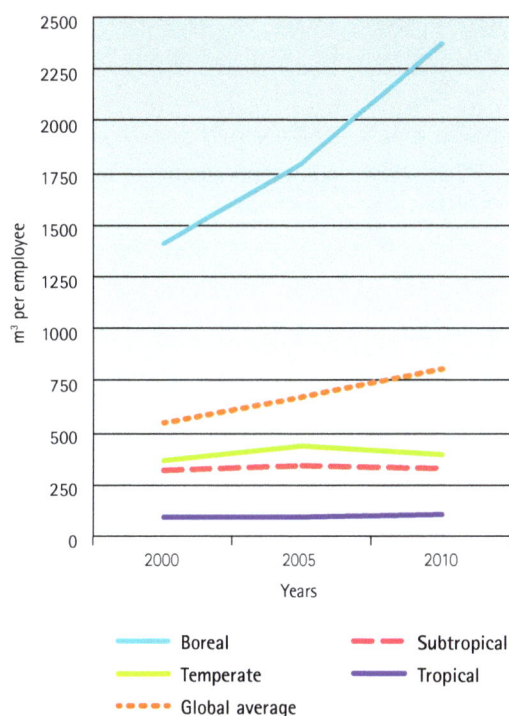

The number of employees per 1 000 ha of forest has increased from 3.0 to 3.1 in the last 20 years. There are large differences among countries, partly explained by the importance of the forest sector at the national level.

Globally, labour productivity (i.e. a worker's output per unit of time) has gradually increased during the last ten years (Figure 30). Productivity has increased as a country's level of economic development has increased. Countries in the tropical domain increased employment and wood removals at similar rates, therefore productivity remains almost unchanged. The opposite happened in countries in the boreal domain where employment decreased at a higher rate than wood removals, thus keeping productivity high through the crisis period 2007–2009.

WHAT IS THE FUTURE OUTLOOK?
Globally, employment in forestry and logging seems likely to decline as productivity increases in most parts of the world. This decline is unlikely to occur in countries with high woodfuel use, where labour-use efficiency is unlikely to change in the foreseeable future.

Forest ownership and management rights

WHY IS THIS INDICATOR IMPORTANT?
Information on who owns the forest and who has forest management rights is critical in tracking environmental, social, and economic development. Clear ownership and management rights are vital for good governance and sustainable management of forests. Information about forest ownership helps us to better understand who controls forest management and use, and who benefits or loses from forest production. When forest tenure is secure, it promotes capital investment by government and the private sector and also has a role in the arrangement of incentives that motivate the sustainable use of forest resources.

WHAT HAS CHANGED AND WHY?
Reporting on ownership has improved and the proportion of private ownership has increased. In 1990, 64 percent of the global forest area was publicly owned, 13 percent was private, 1 percent was of unknown ownership and 23 percent was unreported. In 2010, 74 percent of the global forest area was

publicly owned, 19 percent was private, 4 percent was of unknown ownership and 3 percent was unreported. However, global figures mask the importance of private forest for countries with private forest ownership. For countries that have a mix of private and public forest, the proportion of private forest ownership went from

26 percent in 1990 to 30 percent in 2010. Western and Central Africa is the region with the highest proportion of public ownership (99 percent) followed by Western and Central Asia (98 percent) and South and Southeast Asia (90 percent). The highest proportion of private forest is found in East Asia and Oceania (42 percent), followed by North America (33 percent).

The largest increase in private ownership was observed in the upper middle-income category where the area of private ownership nearly doubled (Figure 31). China accounted for an increase of 85 million ha, mainly as a result of the implementation of the 2008 reform of collective forest ownership.

Between 1990 and 2010 the share of individual ownership of private forests increased from 42 percent in 1990 to 56 percent in 2010 and at the same time the proportion of private forest area owned by private business entities, institutions, and local, tribal and indigenous communities declined. Even though the relative proportion of forest owned by communities has decreased from 19 percent in 1990 to 15 percent in 2010, in real terms the forest area owned by communities has increased from 60 million ha to 64 million ha.

The proportion of publicly-owned forest owned by the state at the national scale decreased from 47 percent of all publicly-owned forest in 1990 to 23 percent in 2010.

FIGURE 31 **Trends in private ownership by income category**

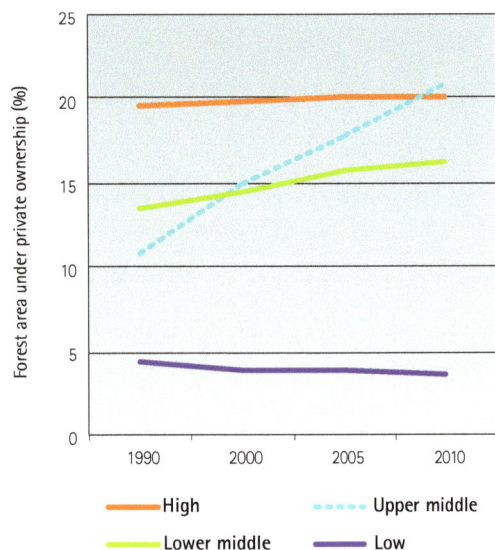

FIGURE 32 **Distribution of private ownership of forest (1990–2010)**

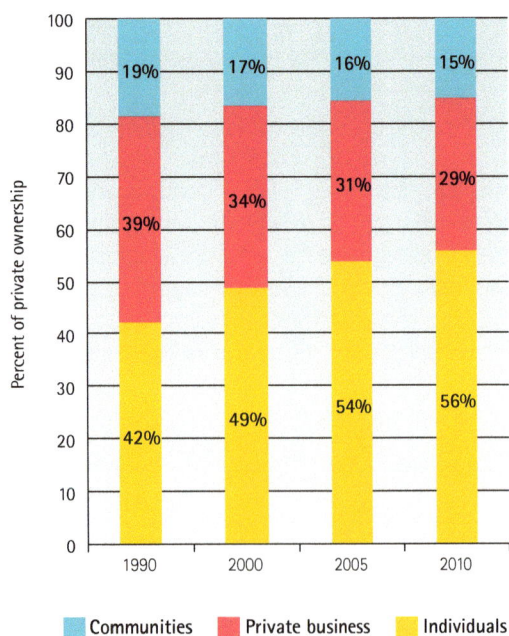

FIGURE 33 **Changes in management rights of publicly-owned forest (1990–2010)**

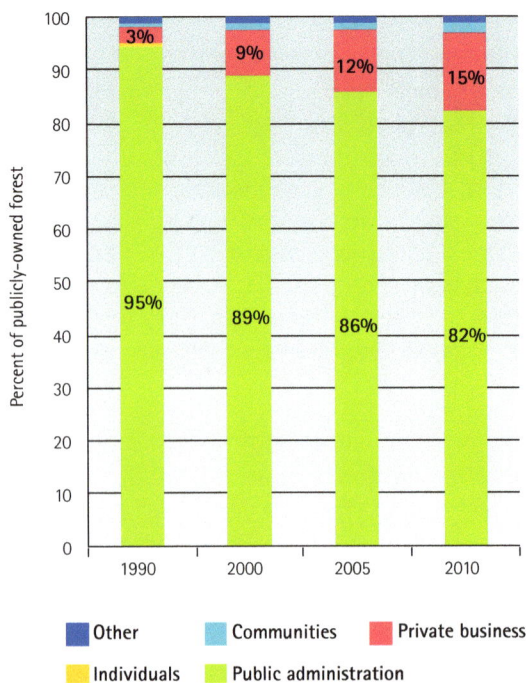

This is largely due to a significant shift in the Russian Federation from national to subnational ownership.

Figure 32 illustrates a steady decline in community and private business ownership and an increase in individual forest ownership.

At the global level, the management rights of publicly-owned forest are dominated by the state with almost 82 percent, followed by private companies at 15 percent (Figure 33). Between 1990 and 2010 the management responsibilities of states decreased from nearly 95 percent in 1990 to almost 82 percent in 2010.

The countries with the largest public forest area under community management were Brazil and Colombia with 152 million ha and 30 million ha respectively. Timor-Leste and Saint Pierre and Miquelon reported having 100 percent of their publicly-owned forest under community management rights.

WHAT IS THE FUTURE OUTLOOK?

The current trend in forest tenure towards increased private ownership, and private companies having increased management responsibilities for public forests, is likely to continue. Likewise, decentralization of forests from national to subnational levels is likely to continue in many countries. Privatization of forests in the upper middle-income countries appears likely to continue, particularly as national incomes increase.

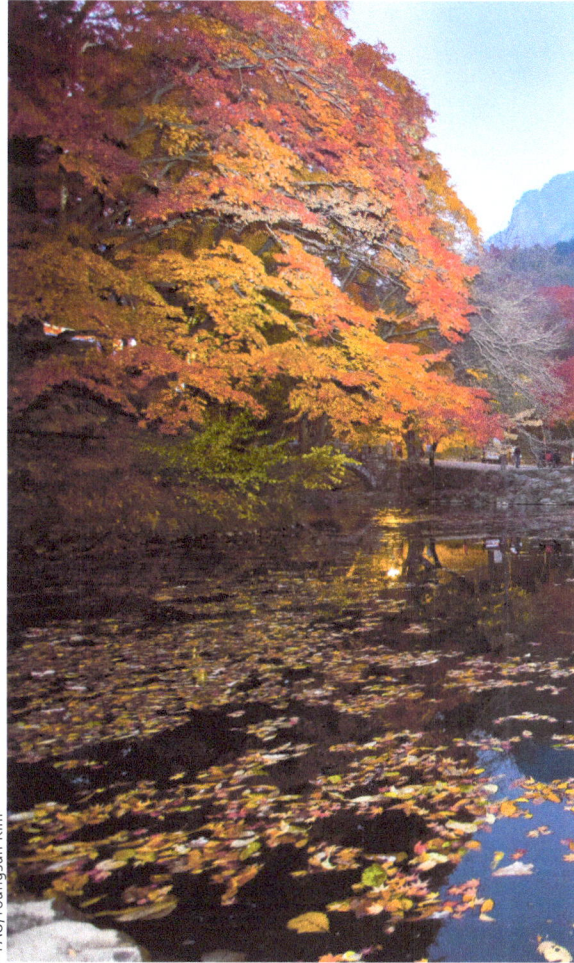

©FAO/Youngsun Kim

Importance of forests in Small Island Developing States

WHY ARE THESE FORESTS IMPORTANT?

Forest cover in Small Island Developing States (SIDS)[12] represents less than 1 percent of the world's forest area, insignificant in global terms. However in many SIDS, forests and trees play a more crucial role in social and economic development than in many larger countries. Many island habitats also have global significance for conservation of biological diversity and particular endemic species.

Forest management is important in SIDS because of the vital role of forest in soil and water protection and disaster risk resilience. In addition, coastal forests and mangrove forests are important for marine habitat and for protection from coastal erosion.

WHAT HAS CHANGED AND WHY?

Small Island Developing States have some of the world's highest forest cover in percentage of land area covered by forest. In fact, six of the top ten countries in proportion of forest to land area are SIDS. Over 25 years the total forest area in SIDS has increased from 80.8 million ha to 82 million ha in 2015.

The five largest forest area countries represent more than 86 percent of the total forest area of SIDS while the 38 smallest countries in terms of forest area represent only 1.6 percent of the forest area (Table 11). While forest area in SIDS countries with the least forest increased from 1990 to 2010, the rate of increase has declined from +11,000 ha in the 1990s to +2 800 in the 2000s. This

cc0/pixabay

---

12 American Samoa, Anguilla, Antigua and Barbuda, Aruba, Bahamas, Bahrain, Barbados, Belize, British Virgin Islands, Cabo Verde, Comoros, Cook Islands, Cuba, Cyprus, Dominica, Dominican Republic, Fiji, French Polynesia, Grenada, Guam, Guinea-Bissau, Guyana, Haiti, Jamaica, Kiribati, Maldives, Malta, Marshall Islands, Mauritius, Micronesia (Fed. States of), Montserrat, Nauru, Netherlands Antilles, New Caledonia, Niue, Northern Mariana Islands, Palau, Papua New Guinea, Puerto Rico, Saint Kitts and Nevis, Saint Lucia, Saint Vincent and the Grenadines, Samoa, Sao Tome and Principe, Seychelles, Singapore, Solomon Islands, Suriname, Timor-Leste, Tonga, Trinidad and Tobago, Tuvalu, United States Virgin Islands, Vanuatu.

TABLE 11 **Small Island Developing States forest area by forest area size class (2015)**

Country forest area class	Number of countries	Forest area (million ha)	% of SIDS forest area
Large (>2 million ha)	5	70.8	86
Medium (200 000 to 2 million ha)	11	9.9	12
Small(<200 000 ha)	38	1.3	2
Total	54	82.0	

FIGURE 34 **Annual change in forest area by income categories**

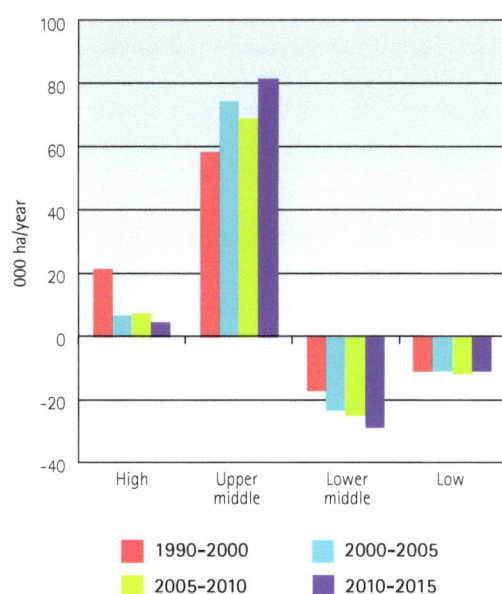

■ 1990–2000 ■ 2000–2005
■ 2005–2010 ■ 2010–2015

FIGURE 35 **Annual change in forest area by forest area categories**

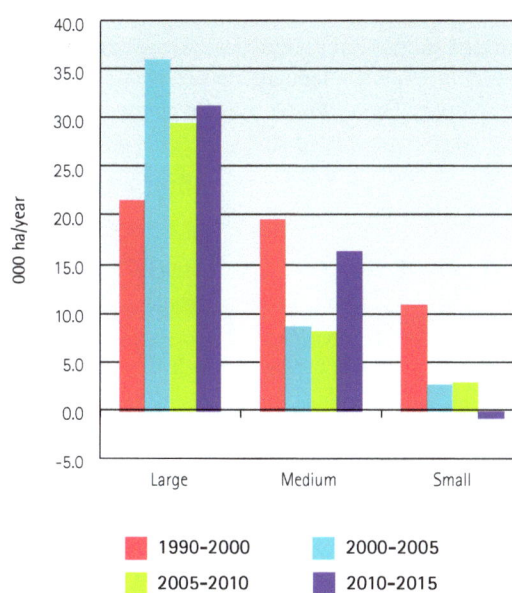

■ 1990–2000 ■ 2000–2005
■ 2005–2010 ■ 2010–2015

changed to a forest area loss of 1 000 ha per year from 2010 to 2015.

The forest area increased in SIDS with large forest areas and in the high- and upper middle-income categories, while lower middle- and low-income category countries (Figure 34) and small forest area countries (Figure 35) showed decreases in forest area.

Thanks to a wide variety of plant species providing habitats for a wealth of animal species, mangrove ecosystems are not only rich in biodiversity but they also serve as protection areas from natural disasters such as cyclones, erosion from sea level rise and tsunamis.

They also provide landscapes that are highly valued for residential and tourism uses. Globally there are almost 15 million ha of mangroves of which about 15 percent (2.2 million ha) are found in SIDS.

WHAT IS THE FUTURE OUTLOOK?

Forests in Small Island Developing States will remain important for biodiversity and socioeconomic values. Forest area change is difficult to predict given the volatility in change rates, but it is unlikely that large changes in area will occur in the near future. The only exception appears to be in the small SIDS where forest area is decreasing; this is an important issue given the loss rates in these countries over the past 25 years.

Looking to the future of forest area change

WHY IS THIS IMPORTANT?

Understanding past forest resource change tells us what presently exists and where change has been important. It does not necessarily tell us what to expect in the future. Human populations, demand for food and forest products, less suitable soils for cultivation and greater access to forested land – all these factors have implications for future forest area. This is true for both conservation and production forest.

WHAT DO WE EXPECT WILL CHANGE?

Changes in forest area differ dramatically by region. Figure 36 shows forest area by region as calculated from FRA data for the period 1990-2010 (solid line); projected from the Global Forest Resources Model (GFRM) towards 2050 (dotted line); and extrapolated from the country specific aspiration for 2030 as reported in FRA 2015 (large dots). South America has the largest proportion of projected forest loss, followed by Africa. Forest in all other regions is projected to increase. Note that the divergence for Asia and Africa is strongly influenced by the low representation of reporting countries and changing trends expected from certain countries within these regions.

South America and North America have the largest areas designated for protection and small projected loss in protected areas. Africa and Asia are projected to suffer the highest portion of protected areas loss (–0.7 percent and –0.9 percent). Subregions with little or no projected loss in areas such as Northern Africa, East Asia and Western and Central Asia have very small protected areas.

©FAO/Jason D'Souza

FIGURE 36 **Projected forest area by region (1990–2050): the solid line is from FRA data, the dotted line is projected from the GFRM and the large dots are country aspirations reported in FRA 2015**

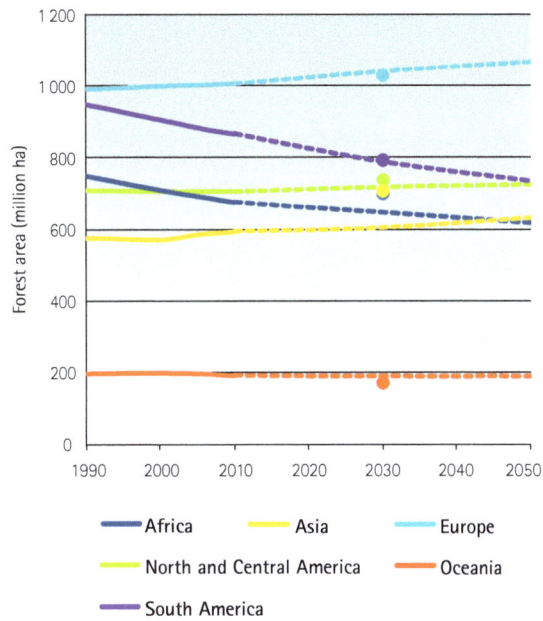

A total of 91 countries indicated their expectations for forest area change to 2030. Most countries (58) indicated that they are expecting the trend to remain the same. Loss is expected in Brazil and Mali and gain is expected in China, India and the Russian Federation. On the other hand, Bhutan, Belarus, the United States of America and the Islamic Republic of Iran had their forest area increase over the past 15 years but expect forest loss in the next 15 years. Conversely, countries such as Argentina, Indonesia, Nepal, Nigeria, Thailand and the United Republic of Tanzania are expecting losses observed in the past to be reversed into forest area gains.

By climatic domain, clearly the greatest risk of forest loss will remain in the tropics, particularly for production forests (Table 12). Risks are lower in the subtropics and very low in the temperate and boreal domains. Protected forest loss follows a similar pattern but at much lower rates.

The forests that remain most at risk of conversion are clearly the production and multiple-use forests within the tropical domain. The forests under protected areas showed relatively little risk of being converted to other land uses in the near future.

TABLE 12 **Projected area of forest at risk of being lost by 2030 within production and protection forests by climatic domain and FRA region**

Area of forest at risk of being lost (2010–2030)		% climatic domains			
		Tropical	Subtropical	Temperate	Boreal
Production forest	Proportion of 2010 production forest	15	5	0.80	0
	Proportion of 2010 total forest area	4	2	0.50	0
Protected forest	Proportion of 2010 protected forest area	3	1	0.10	0
	Proportion of 2010 total forest area	0.30	0.10	0.02	0

Data sources and quality

Most of the data reported in this and other FRA 2015 publications come from Country Reports prepared by national governments. These reports are generally prepared by a national correspondent and are reviewed by national forest authorities according to national regulations or practice.

FRA 2015 provides reports on 234 countries and territories, of which 155 come from Country Reports prepared by national correspondents nominated by government agencies responsible for forestry. The remainder come from desk studies, which since FRA 2000 have been used to provide estimated values for forest statistics in countries or territories that have not nominated a national correspondent or have not provided a country report. While the number of desk studies is high, in total they represent only 1.2 percent of global

forest area. This means that for FRA 2015, 98.8 percent of global forest area has been reported by the countries themselves.

Data collection and reporting leading up to 2015 was guided by a series of workshops and training sessions designed to maximize consistency between reports. This was assisted for FRA 2015 by the online data collection portal, the Forest Resources Information Management System (FRIMS). Countries were provided with pre-filled templates that incorporated their values from 1990 to 2010 as per their submissions to FRA 2010.

Countries were requested to revise former figures and update them when new data were available and then estimate the figures for 2015. This allows countries to update previous reports when new data have become

available. In addition to the data reported by countries, FAO has worked with national correspondents in providing data assembled from other sources. Most of these are sources previously provided by national governments to the United Nations, including data on population, land area and wood removals.

It is important to note that all Country Reports were independently peer-reviewed by FAO staff, partners in the Collaborative Forest Resources Questionnaire (CFRQ) and external experts. Peer-review comments were provided to national correspondents for inclusion and, where necessary, corrections of individual national reports were made before incorporation of data into the final FRA 2015 database.

The reporting format for countries encourages them to provide data for references and calculations. In some cases, countries have provided excellent documentation that allows the reader to examine and recalculate values submitted for FRA 2015. Readers may refer to the Country Reports for details, references and descriptions.[13] That website also has publications and documents describing terms and definitions, and the guide to FRA 2015.

FRA 2015 used a set of tier categories similar to those used by the Intergovernmental Panel on Climate Change (IPCC). Tiers were requested for all variables that potentially had more than one source of data. Tiers were defined by countries for each of the included variables for both status (i.e. the most recent report) and trend (i.e. for two or more reporting periods). Countries were asked to assign a tier value to each qualifying variable: Tier 1 (expert estimate), Tier 2 (low intensity or incomplete surveys, older data) or Tier 3 (high reliability, recent sources with national scope). Specific definitions for each tier were provided in the FRIMS following this general pattern and are available in the FRA Country Reports online.

13 See www.fao.org/forestry/fra2015.

References

FAO. 2010. *Global Forest Resources Assessment 2010*. Rome (available at www.fao.org/forestry/fra/fra2010/en/).

FAO. 2012. *FRA 2015. Terms and Definitions*. Forest Resources Assessment Working Paper 180. Rome (available at http://www.fao.org/docrep/017/ap862e/ap862e00.pdf).

FAO. 2014. *State of the World's Forests 2014*. Rome(available at www.fao.org/forestry/sofo/en/).

FAO. *Country Reports*. Rome (available at www.fao.org/forestry/fra2015).

Fernholz, K. & Kraxner, F. 2012. Certified forest products markets, 2011-2012. In *UNECE/FAO Forest Products Annual Market Review*. Geneva, United Nations Economic Commission for Europe (available at www.unece.org/fileadmin/DAM/timber/publications/10.pdf).

ISIC. 2008. *International Standard Industrial Classification of All Economic Activities (ISIC), Rev. 4*. Statistical Papers Series M, No, 4, Rev. 4. New York, United Nations (available at unstats.un.org/unsd/publication/seriesM/seriesm_4rev4e.pdf).

United Nations General Assembly. Resolution A/RES/62/98, 31 January 2008. New York, United Nations.

www.ingramcontent.com/pod-product-compliance
Lightning Source LLC
Chambersburg PA
CBHW060856270326
41934CB00003B/164